Beyond the Checkered Flag:
The Story of McLaren vs. Ferrari

Etienne Psaila

Beyond the Checkered Flag: The Story of McLaren vs. Ferrari

Copyright © 2024 by Etienne Psaila. All rights reserved.

This Edition: **March 2024**

No part of this publication may be reproduced, distributed, or transmitted in any form or by any means, including photocopying, recording, or other electronic or mechanical methods, without the prior written permission of the publisher, except in the case of brief quotations embodied in critical reviews and certain other non-commercial uses permitted by copyright law.

This book is part of the 'Automotive and Motorcycle Books' series and each volume in the series is crafted with respect for the automotive and motorcycle brands discussed, utilizing brand names and related materials under the principles of fair use for educational purposes. The aim is to celebrate and inform, providing readers with a deeper appreciation for the engineering marvels and historical significance of these iconic brands.

Cover design by Etienne Psaila
Interior layout by Etienne Psaila

Website: www.etiennepsaila.com
Contact: etipsaila@gmail.com

Table of Contents

Chapter 1: The Starting Line

Chapter 2: Titans of the Track

Chapter 3: Engineering Excellence

Chapter 4: The Duel Begins

Chapter 5: Speed and Strategy

Chapter 6: Clashes and Controversies

Chapter 7: The Psychology of Racing

Chapter 8: Triumphs and Trophies

Chapter 9: Innovations and Accusations

Chapter 10: Legends Behind the Wheel

Chapter 11: The New Era

Chapter 12: Beyond the Track

Chapter 13: The Checkered Flag

Chapter 1: The Starting Line

The sun had barely risen over the sleepy town of Maranello, Italy, but the air was already thick with anticipation. In the heart of this unassuming locale stood the headquarters of Scuderia Ferrari, a name that echoed through the halls of automotive history with the weight of passion, triumph, and tragedy. Just over a thousand kilometers away, in Woking, UK, the McLaren Technology Centre, an architectural marvel reflecting the blend of innovation and tradition, hummed with activity. Here, nestled amidst the Surrey countryside, another titan of Formula 1 prepared to write the next chapter in a storied rivalry.

The roots of this feud were as much a part of Formula 1's fabric as the checkered flag that marked its races' ends. To understand it, one had to delve into the annals of motor racing history, back to when Formula 1 emerged from the ashes of World War II as the pinnacle of automotive competition. It was a sport where human courage met engineering brilliance on asphalt battlegrounds, carving heroes and villains out of men and machines.

Enzo Ferrari, the enigmatic founder of the Ferrari racing team, was already a legend by the time Bruce McLaren, a determined and talented New Zealander, decided to challenge the European racing establishment by forming his own team. Enzo, with his dark sunglasses perpetually masking his gaze, was as much a sorcerer conjuring magic from his cars as he was a shrewd businessman. Bruce McLaren, on the other hand, brought a pioneering spirit, an engineer's mind, and the relentless pursuit of excellence to the table. The stage was set for a clash of titans.

The early days of Formula 1 were marked by raw power, dangerous circuits, and a fraternity of drivers who raced with death shadowing their every turn. McLaren and Ferrari, however, were not just racing against each other; they were racing against the very limits of human and mechanical endurance. Each victory, each loss was a note in the symphony of their rivalry.

As the sport evolved, so did the nature of this contest. It was no longer just about who could build the fastest car or who dared push the limits of physical endurance further. It became a battle of wits, strategy, and technology. The introduction of aerodynamics, turbocharging, and electronic aids transformed the cars into high-speed computers on wheels, and the rivalry between McLaren and Ferrari into a chess match at over 200 miles per hour.

But the heart of this story was not just in the technology or the tactics; it was in the people. Men like Ayrton Senna and Alain Prost for McLaren, and Niki Lauda and Michael Schumacher for Ferrari, became the avatars of their teams' aspirations, their triumphs, and their tragedies on the track. Their battles, both on and off the circuit, were punctuated by moments of sheer brilliance, devastating heartbreak, and, occasionally, controversy.

In the paddocks, amidst the roar of engines and the smell of burning rubber, stories of rivalry, friendship, innovation, and courage unfolded. These were the tales that defined the essence of the McLaren-Ferrari feud, a narrative that transcended the realm of sports to become a testament to human passion and perseverance.

As the world of Formula 1 raced into the 21st century, the rivalry between McLaren and Ferrari remained as fierce as ever, fueled by new stars, evolving technologies, and the undiminished desire to claim the mantle of the world's premier racing team. The starting line of this story was drawn decades ago, but the race, it seemed, was far from over.

Chapter 2: Titans of the Track

In the grand theater of Formula 1, where technology and human ambition converge at the zenith of motorsport, few roles are as pivotal as those of the drivers, engineers, and managers. These are the craftsmen of speed, the architects of victory, and the strategists of the asphalt. In the tale of McLaren versus Ferrari, each team boasted figures of legendary stature, whose contributions not only defined their era but also sculpted the very legacy of the sport.

McLaren: The Visionaries

Bruce McLaren

In the heart of the 1960s, a period of revolutionary change and boundless optimism, a young New Zealander named Bruce McLaren dared to envision a future where his name would become synonymous with racing excellence and technological innovation. Bruce, with his sandy hair often tousled by the wind and eyes alight with a mixture of determination and an ever-present spark of mischief, was not your typical Formula 1 driver. He possessed a rare blend of talents: a gifted racer, an ingenious engineer, and, most importantly, a visionary leader.

Bruce's journey from the racetracks of New Zealand to the pinnacle of Formula 1 is a testament to his unwavering commitment to his dream. Standing at the garage, clad in his racing overalls that bore the marks of oil and the rigors of racing, Bruce would often be found deep in conversation with his team, his hands animated as he described his latest idea to improve the car's performance. "We're not here just to participate," he'd say, his voice carrying the weight of his aspirations, "we're here to innovate, to lead, and to win."

His approach to racing was revolutionary. Bruce believed that to be truly competitive, one had to understand the machine as intimately as the self. This belief led him to become deeply involved in the design and engineering of his cars, a rarity among drivers of his time. His teammate and friend, Tyler, recalled a moment that epitomized Bruce's dedication: "There was Bruce, hours after everyone had left, still at the workshop, poring over the blueprints and models. He had this incredible ability to see not just what the car was, but what it could become."

Tragically, Bruce's brilliant career was cut short in 1970 during a testing accident at Goodwood. The news sent shockwaves through the racing world. The loss of Bruce McLaren was not just a blow to his team but to the entire motorsport community. In the days following the accident, the McLaren team gathered, the air heavy with grief and uncertainty. It was in this moment of despair that Bruce's ethos shone brightest. "Bruce wouldn't have wanted us to give up," declared Teddy Mayer, his voice steady but filled with emotion. "We owe it to him to continue, to realize his vision of what McLaren can be."

And continue they did. Under Bruce's guiding ethos of innovation, determination, and courage, McLaren evolved from a fledgling team into a Formula 1 powerhouse. The team's resilience in the face of adversity and commitment to pushing the boundaries of technology became its hallmark, a tribute to the legacy of their founder.

Today, McLaren stands as a testament to Bruce McLaren's vision. The team's pursuit of excellence on and off the track echoes his belief in the power of innovation and the spirit of competition. Bruce's legacy lives on in every car that bears his name, in every race they compete, and in the hearts of those who continue to be inspired by his story. "Bruce McLaren taught us that to achieve the impossible, one must first believe it to be possible," remarked a current McLaren engineer, reflecting on the enduring impact of the team's founder.

Bruce McLaren's story is not just about racing; it's about the relentless pursuit of dreams against all odds. It's a narrative that continues to inspire a new generation of drivers, engineers, and dreamers to push the limits of what's possible, guided by the star of innovation, determination, and courage that Bruce set alight in the world of Formula 1.

Ron Dennis

In the vibrant tapestry of Formula 1, few figures have woven as indelible a pattern as Ron Dennis. Taking the helm of McLaren in the 1980s, Dennis was not merely stepping into a leadership role; he was embarking on a mission to redefine what a racing team could be. With a demeanor as sharp as the suits he invariably wore, Dennis brought an almost surgical precision to the chaotic world of motorsport. His piercing gaze seemed to look through the present, envisioning a future where McLaren was not just participating in Formula 1 but dominating it.

Dennis's approach to leadership was both revolutionary and uncompromising. He viewed McLaren as a diamond in the rough, brimming with potential but in need of refinement. "Excellence is a habit, not an act," he would often say, a mantra that became the team's guiding principle. Under his stewardship, McLaren's headquarters transformed into a temple of innovation and efficiency, embodying the ethos of its leader.

The impact of Dennis's meticulous nature was felt in every facet of the team. Meetings were legendary for their intensity and attention to detail. Engineers and designers found in Dennis a demanding but visionary leader, one who could challenge them to push beyond their limits. "Ron doesn't just expect perfection, he demands it," recounted a senior engineer, recalling late nights spent refining every component, every strategy, down to the minutest detail.

Dennis's strategic acumen was matched by his commitment to nurturing talent. He had an eye for spotting potential, not just among drivers but within the ranks of engineers, mechanics, and support staff. Legends like Ayrton Senna and Alain Prost flourished under his regime, drawn not only by McLaren's competitive edge but by the culture of excellence that Dennis instilled. In the heat of competition, Dennis remained a stoic figure, his calm demeanor belying the fierce competitive spirit that drove him.

The era of dominance that McLaren enjoyed under Ron Dennis's leadership was no accident. It was the result of relentless pursuit of perfection, a philosophy that permeated every aspect of the team's operations. Championships were not just won on the track but in the countless hours of preparation, analysis, and innovation that defined McLaren's approach.

Yet, for all his achievements, Dennis remained a figure of humility. "I am but one chapter in the McLaren story," he once remarked, acknowledging the collective effort of his team. His legacy, however, speaks volumes of his impact—not just in the trophies and accolades but in the very ethos of McLaren, a testament to the transformative power of vision, discipline, and unwavering commitment to excellence.

As Formula 1 continues to evolve, the influence of Ron Dennis on McLaren and the sport as a whole remains a benchmark of leadership. In the pursuit of victory, Dennis's mantra of excellence echoes as a reminder that the path to greatness is paved with attention to detail, strategic vision, and an unrelenting demand for perfection.

Ayrton Senna

In the tempestuous world of Formula 1 during the late 1980s and early 1990s, a figure emerged whose name would become synonymous with the very essence of racing: Ayrton Senna. Joining McLaren, Senna brought with him not just exceptional driving skills but an intense, almost spiritual approach to the sport. His lean frame, intense gaze beneath the brim of his racing helmet, and the calm, measured tone of his voice belied a fierce competitor with an insatiable desire to be the best.

Senna's arrival at McLaren coincided with the team's ascendancy in the Formula 1 world, a period marked by innovation and rivalry. From the outset, it was clear that Senna was not a driver content with merely competing; he sought to redefine the limits of what was possible on the racetrack. His work ethic was unparalleled, often seen discussing tire pressures, aerodynamics, and engine settings with his engineers late into the night. "There is always a way to go faster," he'd assert, poring over telemetry data to find the smallest margins for improvement.

The rivalry with his teammate Alain Prost would come to

define Senna's tenure at McLaren. Two titans of the sport, their battles on the track were epic, a compelling drama that captivated fans worldwide. Yet, it was their contrasting styles and personalities that added depth to their rivalry. Prost, the professor, was calculated and strategic, while Senna, the artist, combined raw speed with a daring, almost reckless bravery. Their duels, particularly the infamous clashes at Suzuka in 1988 and 1989, were more than races; they were philosophical debates at 200 miles per hour, each driver testing the other's limits and their own.

Despite the intensity of their rivalry, there was a mutual respect between Senna and Prost, an acknowledgment of the other's talent and dedication to the sport. "We are different," Senna once mused in an interview, his voice reflective, "but we have a common goal—to be the best." This rivalry pushed both drivers to heights previously unseen in Formula 1, their quest for perfection elevating the entire sport.

Senna's commitment to excellence was evident not just in his quest for victories but in his approach to life. He was deeply philosophical, often speaking about the connection between his mind, body, and the machine he piloted. To Senna, racing was more than a competition; it was a means of exploring the limits of human potential. "When I race, I feel something beyond just the physical," he confided, "I tap into a place where everything is in harmony."

His untimely death at the San Marino Grand Prix in 1994 left the world of motorsport in mourning, a stark reminder of the risks these drivers take in their pursuit of glory. Yet, Senna's legacy endures, not just in the record books but in the hearts of fans and fellow drivers. His relentless pursuit of perfection, his profound connection to the act of racing, and his legendary rivalry with Prost have become integral chapters in the story of Formula 1.

Ayrton Senna's time with McLaren remains a golden era for the team, a period marked by triumph, tragedy, and the unyielding spirit of competition. His life and career continue to inspire, a testament to the power of dedication, passion, and the relentless pursuit of excellence.

Adrian Newey

In the high-octane world of Formula 1, where engineering prowess is just as critical as driving skill, Adrian Newey emerged as a figure whose visionary designs would redefine the landscape of the sport. In the 1990s, Newey, with his distinctive blend of creativity and technical acumen, became a pivotal force behind McLaren's resurgence as a dominant force in Formula 1.

Newey, often seen with his trademark pens and sketchpad in hand, was more than just an aerodynamicist; he was an artist whose medium was air itself. His tall, slight frame and contemplative demeanor belied a mind always at work, constantly iterating over the fluid dynamics that govern high-speed racing. His colleagues at McLaren would often find him in the depths of thought, sketching intricate designs that would later become the hallmark of McLaren's championship-winning cars.

"Form follows function, but that doesn't mean it can't be beautiful," Newey would remark, his eyes lighting up as he described the philosophy behind his designs. This ethos became evident in the sleek lines and innovative aerodynamic features of the McLaren cars of the 1990s. Under Newey's guidance, the team introduced groundbreaking concepts that not only enhanced performance but also set new standards in aesthetics.

One of Newey's most significant contributions was his ability to balance the quest for aerodynamic efficiency with the stringent regulatory changes that often challenge Formula 1 designers. His designs were a masterclass in innovation within constraints, finding performance gains in areas others overlooked. "It's like solving a complex puzzle," Newey explained during a team meeting, outlining his approach to designing within the ever-evolving rules of Formula 1.

Newey's tenure at McLaren was marked by a series of triumphant seasons, with drivers benefiting from his relentless pursuit of aerodynamic perfection. The team's drivers, encased in the cockpit of Newey's creations, often spoke of the confidence his cars inspired on the track. "Driving one of Adrian's cars is like having a conversation with the road," one McLaren driver said, reflecting on the intuitive handling and responsiveness that were trademarks of a Newey-designed vehicle.

Despite the pressures and the fast-paced environment of Formula 1, Newey remained a figure of calm determination, always focused on the next innovation, the next leap forward. His legacy at McLaren is not just the championships won or the races dominated but the influence he had on the sport's approach to design and engineering. Newey's work challenged his peers and successors to think differently about how cars are built, how air can be sculpted, and how beauty and speed are not mutually exclusive.

Adrian Newey's impact on McLaren and Formula 1 as a whole is a testament to the power of visionary thinking and creative engineering. As Formula 1 continues to evolve, the principles and innovations introduced by Newey remain a benchmark for excellence, a reminder that at the intersection of science and artistry lies the potential to revolutionize the very nature of speed.

Ferrari: The Prancing Horse

Enzo Ferrari

In the annals of motorsport history, few names resonate as powerfully as that of Enzo Ferrari, a man whose life was inextricably linked with the very essence of racing. Born in Modena, Italy, Enzo's journey from a modest beginning to the pinnacle of automotive and motorsport excellence is a testament to his indomitable spirit, unwavering passion, and deep understanding of what it takes to win.

Enzo Ferrari, often seen in his iconic dark sunglasses and with a reserved demeanor, possessed a fiery passion for racing that burned beneath his composed exterior. His early experiences as a driver laid the foundation for what would become the ethos of Ferrari: a relentless pursuit of perfection and a deep-seated belief in the spirit of competition. "The most important victory is the one yet to come," Enzo would often say, encapsulating his forward-looking perspective and insatiable appetite for success.

Under his leadership, Ferrari evolved from a small racing team into a symbol of Italian pride and a bastion of motorsport excellence. The Ferrari Scuderia, adorned with the prancing horse, became more than just a team; it was a manifestation of Enzo's dreams and aspirations, a beacon for like-minded individuals drawn to the allure of speed and the pursuit of victory.

Enzo's understanding of what it took to win was not limited to the technical aspects of building racing cars. He knew that to achieve greatness, one must foster a team spirit infused with passion, dedication, and a collective belief in the mission. "A car is only as good as the team behind it," Enzo remarked, emphasizing the importance of unity and collaboration in the face of competition.

His leadership style was characterized by an unyielding demand for excellence and an intuitive understanding of people. He was a master at motivating his drivers and engineers, pushing them to exceed their own expectations. Legends like Juan Manuel Fangio, Niki Lauda, and Michael Schumacher, who all drove under the Ferrari banner, were not only drawn to the team by the prospect of victory but also by the chance to be part of Enzo's vision.

The legacy of Enzo Ferrari extends far beyond the countless victories and championships. It lies in the emotional connection that millions of fans around the world have with the Ferrari brand. For many, Ferrari is not just a name on a car; it is a symbol of aspiration, an embodiment of the racing spirit, and a testament to the enduring power of dreams. Enzo's life work transformed Ferrari into a living legend, a narrative woven into the fabric of motorsport history.

Today, long after Enzo's passing, his spirit continues to guide Ferrari. His passion for racing, his understanding of victory's price, and his vision for his team remain at the heart of

Ferrari's ethos. Enzo Ferrari's legacy is not just in the cars that bear his name or the trophies in the cabinet; it's in the indelible mark he left on the world of motorsport, inspiring generations to dream big, pursue their passions, and never forget that the most important victory is always the next one.

Luca di Montezemolo

In the early 1990s, Ferrari found itself at a crossroads, grappling with a period of underperformance that threatened to tarnish its storied legacy in Formula 1. It was during this pivotal time that Luca di Montezemolo, with his charismatic presence and visionary leadership, stepped in to steer the Scuderia back to its winning ways. Tall, with an authoritative yet approachable demeanor, Montezemolo possessed an innate understanding of the Ferrari ethos, blending a respect for tradition with a keen eye for innovation and change.

Montezemolo's approach to revitalizing Ferrari was multifaceted. He recognized that success in the modern era of Formula 1 required not just engineering excellence but also strategic acumen and a strong team culture. "We must honor our past," Montezemolo would often say, "but we cannot be afraid to change to win." This philosophy became the cornerstone of his tenure, guiding Ferrari's resurgence as a dominant force in the sport.

Under his leadership, Ferrari underwent significant transformations, both on and off the track. Montezemolo championed the development of cutting-edge technologies while ensuring that the cars remained true to Ferrari's identity as symbols of speed and Italian craftsmanship. He was instrumental in forging partnerships that brought fresh perspectives and expertise to the team, most notably persuading Michael Schumacher, a rising star in the racing world, to join Ferrari.

Montezemolo's leadership style was marked by his ability to inspire and motivate those around him. He was known for his hands-on approach, often seen walking the factory floor, engaging with engineers, and sharing moments of camaraderie with the drivers. His passion was infectious, igniting a renewed sense of purpose and dedication within the team. "Our goal is not just to compete; it is to excel," he would remind his team, pushing them to aim higher, to innovate, and to reclaim Ferrari's position at the pinnacle of Formula 1.

The impact of Montezemolo's tenure at Ferrari was profound.

Under his guidance, the team enjoyed a renaissance, clinching multiple Constructors' and Drivers' Championships and re-establishing Ferrari as a beacon of excellence in Formula 1. But beyond the trophies and accolades, Montezemolo's legacy at Ferrari is encapsulated in the renewed spirit and determination he instilled in the Scuderia.

Luca di Montezemolo's leadership saw Ferrari navigate through one of its most challenging periods, emerging stronger and more focused. By embracing modernity while staying true to Ferrari's rich heritage, he ensured that the Prancing Horse continued to gallop at the forefront of motorsport, embodying the timeless allure and competitive edge that have defined Ferrari for generations. His tenure is a testament to the power of visionary leadership and the enduring spirit of innovation that drives Formula 1 forward.

Michael Schumacher

In the mid-1990s, the world of Formula 1 witnessed a transformative moment that would redefine the legacy of one of its most illustrious teams. Michael Schumacher, a driver already on the path to greatness, made the pivotal decision to join Ferrari, a team with a storied history but in the throes of a competitive drought. With Schumacher's arrival, Ferrari embarked on a journey that would lead to one of the most dominant eras in the sport's history.

Schumacher, with his intense gaze and a physique honed for the rigors of racing, brought to Ferrari not just raw speed but a depth of technical insight and a relentless pursuit of excellence. His approach to racing was methodical, leaving no stone unturned in his quest to extract every ounce of performance from his car. Schumacher's work ethic became the stuff of legend within the paddock; he was often the first to arrive and the last to leave, his dedication inspiring those around him. "To achieve greatness, one must live and breathe racing," Schumacher once remarked, encapsulating his all-encompassing commitment to his craft.

Under the guidance of team principal Jean Todt and with the technical wizardry of designer Rory Byrne, Schumacher became the linchpin of Ferrari's resurgence. His partnership with the team was symbiotic, with Schumacher pushing Ferrari to innovate and Ferrari providing Schumacher with the machinery to showcase his extraordinary talents. Together, they embarked on a meticulous process of improvement, focusing on every aspect of performance, from aerodynamics to engine reliability, from tire strategies to pit stop efficiency.

The results of this relentless pursuit of perfection were soon evident on the track. Schumacher's first championship with Ferrari in 2000, after a 21-year drought for the team, was a cathartic moment, celebrated not just in Maranello but across Italy and around the world. It was a victory that transcended the sport, symbolizing the return of the Prancing Horse to the zenith of Formula 1.

Schumacher's influence extended beyond the confines of the cockpit. He was a leader who led by example, his determination and resilience becoming a rallying cry for the team. "When Michael speaks, we listen," a Ferrari engineer said, "because we know he speaks from the heart and for the good of Ferrari." Schumacher's years at Ferrari were marked by an extraordinary camaraderie and a shared vision of success, the echoes of which continue to resonate within the team.

The golden era heralded by Schumacher's arrival at Ferrari saw the team secure multiple world championships, redefining what was possible in Formula 1. His legacy, however, is measured not just in trophies and records but in the indomitable spirit he instilled in Ferrari. Schumacher's unmatched skill, combined with his unparalleled work ethic, transformed the team and left an indelible mark on the sport.

Today, as Ferrari continues to compete at the highest levels of Formula 1, the ethos of excellence and determination that Schumacher brought to the team remains a cornerstone of its identity. Michael Schumacher's tenure at Ferrari is a testament to the transformative power of a single individual's dedication and passion, inspiring future generations to aspire to greatness, both on and off the track.

Ross Brawn

In the tapestry of Formula 1's storied history, the partnership between Ross Brawn and Michael Schumacher at Ferrari is woven with threads of strategic genius, technical mastery, and unparalleled success. Ross Brawn, a figure synonymous with strategic acumen and engineering excellence, became the architect behind Ferrari's dominance during the Schumacher era, crafting a legacy that is celebrated to this day.

With a demeanor that was calm and contemplative, Brawn's

presence in the Ferrari garage was both commanding and reassuring. His keen analytical mind and profound understanding of the intricacies of Formula 1 racing allowed him to devise strategies that often left competitors trailing in Ferrari's wake. Brawn's approach to race strategy was holistic, considering not just the performance on the track but every variable that could influence the outcome of a race. "Every race is a chess match," Brawn would explain, his voice steady and confident, "and our job is to stay several moves ahead."

Brawn's partnership with Michael Schumacher was based on mutual respect and a shared relentless pursuit of victory. The two formed an almost telepathic understanding, with Brawn's strategic planning complementing Schumacher's driving prowess. Together, they turned race weekends into masterclasses of strategy and execution, their collaboration yielding an era of dominance that is unrivaled in the sport's history.

One of Brawn's most notable contributions to Ferrari's success was his innovative approach to race strategy, particularly in managing pit stops and tire strategies, areas that were often the deciding factors in races. Brawn had a knack for reading the race's flow, making pivotal decisions that could turn the tide in Ferrari's favor. His strategies were not just about reacting to the race conditions but anticipating changes and adapting swiftly to seize the advantage.

Beyond the strategic genius, Brawn's influence extended to the development of the car itself. Working closely with the engineering team, Brawn pushed for innovations that kept Ferrari at the technological forefront of Formula 1. His ability to bridge the gap between the technical and strategic aspects of the sport was a key factor in Ferrari's success, ensuring that the team's efforts on the track were matched by continuous development behind the scenes.

Brawn's legacy at Ferrari is not just the championships won but the culture of excellence and innovation he helped foster. His tenure at Ferrari is remembered as a golden era, a period when strategic brilliance and engineering excellence combined to bring the Scuderia to the zenith of Formula 1. "Our success was born out of collaboration, out of trusting each other and sharing a common goal," Brawn reflected, highlighting the teamwork and unity that were hallmarks of Ferrari's dominance.

Today, as new chapters are written in the annals of Formula 1, the partnership between Ross Brawn and Michael Schumacher remains a benchmark of success. It stands as a testament to the power of strategic thinking, technical innovation, and the unyielding desire to win, principles that continue to inspire and guide teams in their quest for glory in the high-stakes world of Formula 1 racing.

Each of these titans brought their unique strengths to the track—be it through their driving, their vision, or their technical expertise. But beyond their individual contributions, it was their ability to inspire those around them, to push the limits of what was thought possible, and to etch their names into the annals of history that set them apart. The battles they fought, the races they won and lost, and the moments they shared have become the lore of Formula 1.

As the narrative of McLaren and Ferrari unfolded over the decades, these figures stood at the forefront, driving their teams to new heights. Their legacy, however, is not just in the trophies they amassed or the records they broke. It lies in the spirit of competition, the relentless pursuit of excellence, and the passion for speed that they embodied. They were not just titans of the track; they were the very soul of Formula 1, the architects of a rivalry that captured the imagination of fans around the world.

In the next chapters, we delve deeper into the crucible of competition, exploring how these individuals and their teams navigated the challenges of innovation, strategy, and human emotion to write their stories in the fast lanes of Formula 1 history.

Chapter 3: Engineering Excellence

In the heart of Formula 1, where the battle for supremacy is as much about ingenuity as it is about speed, McLaren and Ferrari stood as colossuses, driven by an unquenchable thirst for technological advancement. The rivalry between these two titans was not just fought on racetracks but also in the secretive, hallowed halls of their respective engineering departments. It was here, amid the clatter of keyboards and the hum of wind tunnels, that the future of racing was shaped.

The Aerodynamic Revolution

The dawn of the Aerodynamic Revolution in Formula 1 marked a turning point where science, art, and ambition converged on the racetrack, heralding a new era of competition that was as much about intellect as it was about speed. In this transformative period, two figures stood out as pioneers, their workshops resembling alchemists' labs where the future of racing was being forged: Adrian Newey at McLaren and Ross Brawn at Ferrari.

In the dimly lit confines of his office, surrounded by the skeletal forms of model cars and walls adorned with complex fluid dynamics equations, Adrian Newey was the embodiment of focused innovation. With his pencil perpetually tucked behind his ear and his eyes scanning over the curves of a new design, Newey was a figure of quiet intensity. The late hours of the night often found him and his team huddled over drafting tables, the air thick with the scent of marker ink and the soft hum of computational simulations running in the background.

"We're on the cusp of something revolutionary," Newey would say, his voice a soft but compelling force that drew his team into his vision. "We have the opportunity to redefine what a racing car can be. It's about bending the air to our will, crafting an envelope of speed that clings to the road as if it were part of it." His masterpiece, the MP4/13, was a testament to this philosophy. With its sleek lines and innovative aerodynamic features, the car was a predator on the asphalt, its dominance a tribute to Newey's genius and his team's dedication.

Miles away, in the heart of Maranello, Ross Brawn was steering Ferrari's aerodynamic endeavors with a mix of tactical genius and a deep respect for the Scuderia's heritage. The atmosphere in Ferrari's design office was electric, a sense of history and future potential mingling in the air. Brawn, with his characteristic calm demeanor, stood before his team, the blueprints of the F2002 unfurled before them like a banner.

"This," Brawn declared, pointing to the sleek outlines of the F2002, "represents more than our next race car. It's a symbol of our evolution, a balance of beauty and performance that captures the essence of Ferrari." Under his guidance, the car would go on to achieve legendary status, its design elegantly marrying aerodynamic efficiency with unmatched mechanical grip. Brawn's ability to visualize the airflow around the car, to intuitively understand how each curve and angle would affect performance, made the F2002 a masterpiece of engineering.

The rivalry between McLaren and Ferrari during this era was not just a battle of speed but a duel of wits and innovation. Each Grand Prix became a proving ground for the latest aerodynamic concepts, with Newey and Brawn as the masterminds orchestrating their teams' assaults on the laws of physics.

One memorable moment came during a pre-season test, with both the MP4/13 and the F2002 running laps. As the cars blurred past the main straight, a hush fell over the gathered engineers and drivers, all recognizing the significance of this new chapter in Formula 1. Later, in the debrief room, a McLaren engineer turned to a Ferrari counterpart, a rare moment of camaraderie amidst intense competition. "It's incredible, isn't it?" he said, a nod to the marvels both teams had achieved. "We're not just racing teams; we're pioneers on the frontier of what's possible."

The Aerodynamic Revolution in Formula 1, propelled by visionaries like Adrian Newey and Ross Brawn, reshaped the sport in profound ways. Their contributions went beyond championship titles and race victories; they ignited a passion for innovation that continues to drive Formula 1 forward. In the wind tunnels and on the racetracks, the legacy of this era endures, a testament to the relentless pursuit of perfection and the unyielding spirit of competition that defines the pinnacle of motorsport.

The Power Unit Paradigm

As the 21st century dawned, Formula 1 stood on the precipice of a technological revolution that would redefine the very essence of racing. The introduction of hybrid power units heralded a new era, one that demanded a delicate balance between the ferocious energy of combustion engines and the silent, potent force of electrical power. In this landscape of innovation, two giants of the sport, McLaren and Ferrari, embarked on their respective journeys into the unknown, driven by a commitment to excellence and a vision for the future.

Within the walls of McLaren's technology center, a place where innovation is as much the architecture as it is the ethos, the development of the MP4-30 was underway. The car, sleek and imposing even as it sat stationary, was the culmination of countless hours of research, experimentation, and a daring to venture where no team had gone before. Amidst the hum of activity, a McLaren engineer, her eyes alight with the passion that defined the team's pursuit of progress, spoke of the journey. "The MP4-30 represents more than our entry into the hybrid era; it's a symbol of our relentless quest for innovation," she said, her gaze fixed on the intricate web of wires and circuits that cradled the heart of the hybrid power unit. "Yes, we've faced challenges, but with each challenge comes an opportunity to learn, to improve. We're not just racing for today; we're racing for the future."

Meanwhile, in Maranello, the birthplace of countless racing

legends, Ferrari was crafting its response to the hybrid challenge with the SF15-T. The team's facilities, steeped in history yet brimming with cutting-edge technology, were a testament to Ferrari's unique position at the intersection of tradition and innovation. As the first rays of sunlight pierced the morning mist, casting a golden glow over Fiorano, Ferrari's test track, the SF15-T was unveiled. The car, a striking blend of beauty and engineering prowess, was Ferrari's answer to the hybrid era's demands.

A senior Ferrari engineer, his hands still bearing the marks of his labor, shared his thoughts on the SF15-T's significance. "At Ferrari, we embrace change with the same passion we have for racing. The SF15-T is not just a machine; it's the embodiment of our journey into the hybrid era," he proclaimed, pride evident in his voice. "We've harnessed the synergy between combustion and electric power to create something truly special. Ferrari isn't just adapting to this new era; we're setting the pace, driven by our heritage and our vision for the future."

The advent of hybrid technology in Formula 1 was more than a regulatory change; it was a call to innovate, to reimagine the limits of speed and efficiency. McLaren's MP4-30 and Ferrari's

SF15-T were the vanguards of this new era, each a testament to their team's commitment to excellence and innovation. On the track, these hybrid marvels were not just competing against each other; they were racing towards a new horizon, propelled by the spirit of discovery and a shared passion for the future of motorsport.

As the hybrid era unfolds, the contributions of McLaren and Ferrari continue to shape the landscape of Formula 1. Their pioneering efforts in integrating energy recovery systems and mastering the complex dance of mechanical and electrical power are laying the foundation for the future of racing. In the quest for efficiency and performance, McLaren and Ferrari are not just participants; they are leaders, charting the course for the next chapter of Formula 1's storied history.

The Human Element

As the twilight hours wrapped the paddock in a serene quiet, a rare moment of calm in the relentless world of Formula 1, two of the sport's greatest minds found themselves in an unexpected pause. Adrian Newey, with his characteristic thoughtful expression, sat on a stack of tires outside the McLaren garage, his gaze lost in the distance, reflecting on the day's work. Across from him, Ross Brawn, the strategic mastermind behind Ferrari's resurgence, leaned against a tool cart, both of them surrounded by the faint aroma of spent fuel and rubber—a scent that was the lifeblood of their passion.

The paddock was their sanctuary, a place where the roar of engines and the thrill of competition gave way to moments of introspection and camaraderie. "We're pushing each other to the limits, Ross," Newey remarked, breaking the comfortable silence. His voice, though soft, carried the weight of admiration and the acknowledgment of their shared journey in the quest for innovation.

Brawn, his face breaking into a warm smile, nodded in agreement. "That's the beauty of this sport, Adrian. We're rivals on the track, but here, in this moment, we're just two engineers who love what they do." His eyes, reflecting the glow of the setting sun, sparkled with a mixture of respect and a hint of competition. "We're shaping the future, one innovation at a time."

Their conversation wandered through the intricacies of aerodynamics, the challenges of integrating hybrid technologies, and the unyielding pursuit of performance that defined their careers. It was a dialogue that transcended rivalry, a testament to the human element that lay at the heart of Formula 1's technological arms race.

"We're not just competing with machines; we're racing against human ingenuity, against the limits of what we believe is possible," Newey mused, tracing the outline of a winglet with his finger on the tire beside him. "It's a relentless pursuit, but in that pursuit, we find our greatest triumphs."

Brawn, ever the strategist, leaned forward, his eyes alight with the spark of challenge. "And in that pursuit, we redefine the boundaries of this sport. We make it more than a race; we make it a canvas for innovation, a platform where the impossible becomes the starting point for the next breakthrough."

As the sky deepened into shades of dusk, their conversation drew to a close, but the bond forged in the crucible of competition remained. Newey and Brawn, two titans of Formula 1, stood up, their silhouettes etched against the fading light, reminders of the human spirit that drove the sport forward.

"We'll see what tomorrow brings, Ross," Newey said, extending his hand in a gesture of mutual respect.

Brawn clasped it firmly, his smile reflecting a shared anticipation for the challenges ahead. "Indeed, Adrian. The race goes on, and with it, our journey."

In that handshake, under the canopy of the setting sun, lay the essence of Formula 1's aerodynamic revolution and the unspoken acknowledgment that behind every innovation, every breakthrough, stood men and women whose lives were dedicated to the pursuit of excellence. It was their passion, their relentless drive, that fueled the rivalry and pushed the boundaries of what was possible in Formula 1, shaping the future, one innovation at a time.

As the chapter on engineering excellence closes, the narrative of McLaren and Ferrari's rivalry weaves through the corridors of technological innovation, driven by the brilliance of its people. The stage was set not just for races to be won, but for the very future of Formula 1 to be redefined.

Chapter 4: The Duel Begins

The stage was set under the glaring sun of the Belgian Grand Prix, Spa-Francorchamps, in the early 1980s. The circuit, notorious for its sweeping bends and unpredictable weather, was about to witness the ignition of one of Formula 1's most enduring rivalries. The air was charged with anticipation as the McLaren and Ferrari teams prepared for a race that was more than just a contest of speed—it was the beginning of a duel that would span decades.

In the McLaren garage, the atmosphere was tense but focused. Mechanics swarmed around the sleek, red and white liveried cars, their hands a blur of precision and urgency. John, a seasoned engineer, turned to his team, his voice barely audible over the din of the engines warming up in the background. "This is it, lads. Every bolt, every sensor, every ounce of fuel—it all counts today. Let's show them what we're made of."

Across the paddock, the Ferrari team operated with a rhythm born of years of tradition mixed with Italian passion. Marco, Ferrari's chief strategist, paced before his crew, his gaze fixed on the scarlet machines that bore the hopes of an entire nation. "Remember, we are not just racing for points today; we are racing for pride. Forza Ferrari!"

As the cars lined up on the grid, the tension was palpable. In the McLaren, sat a young and hungry Alain Prost, his eyes narrow, focused solely on the asphalt ahead. Beside him, in the blood-red Ferrari, was Gilles Villeneuve, a driver whose fearless driving style had earned him the admiration of fans and rivals alike. As the lights went out, the two cars rocketed off the line, their engines screaming in harmony as they hurtled towards the first corner.

The race unfolded with the intensity of a high-speed chess match. Prost and Villeneuve traded places with each pass, their cars mere inches apart at speeds that defied belief. On the pit wall, Ron Dennis and Enzo Ferrari watched with bated breath, their eyes never leaving the track as their drivers pushed themselves and their machines to the limit.

As the laps dwindled, the skies above Spa darkened, and rain began to fall, turning the track into a treacherous ribbon of wet asphalt. Prost's voice crackled over the team radio, his French accent thick with concentration. "The conditions are getting worse. I'm switching to wets on the next lap."

In the Ferrari garage, the decision was made to keep Villeneuve out on slick tires, a gamble that could win the race or end in disaster. Marco's voice was firm as he relayed the decision. "Gilles, stay out. This is our chance. You can handle it."

The final laps were a masterclass in driving from both Prost and Villeneuve, their cars dancing on the edge of control. As they approached the final turn, side by side, the crowd rose to its feet, the air electric with excitement. With a daring move on the outside, Villeneuve edged ahead, his Ferrari crossing the finish line just ahead of Prost's McLaren.

As the engines cooled and the teams packed away their gear, the significance of the race began to sink in. This was not just another Grand Prix; it was the beginning of a rivalry that would define Formula 1 for years to come. The respect between Prost and Villeneuve was palpable as they shook hands on the podium, their eyes locking in a silent acknowledgment of the battles that lay ahead.

That day at Spa-Francorchamps, as the champagne flowed and the crowds dispersed, the duel had begun. McLaren and Ferrari, two titans of the track, embarked on a journey of competition, innovation, and passion—a journey that would take them to the very pinnacle of motor racing, forging a rivalry that was as much about the people behind the machines as it was about the cars themselves.

Chapter 5: Speed and Strategy

The sun had not yet risen over the Principality of Monaco, yet the narrow, winding streets of Monte Carlo were alive with the symphony of racing engines. It was the late 1990s, a pivotal era in the McLaren-Ferrari rivalry, marked by not just the sheer speed of their machines, but the cunning and strategy that guided them. The Monaco Grand Prix, Formula 1's crown jewel, was about to become the stage for a strategic duel that would be remembered for generations.

In the McLaren garage, situated in the tight confines of the Monaco pit lane, the air was thick with concentration. Mika Häkkinen, the team's stoic Finnish driver, sat silently in his car, his ice-blue eyes fixed on the data screen before him. Beside him, Ron Dennis, the McLaren team principal, discussed the race strategy in hushed tones with his lead strategist, Tom. "It's all about precision here," Ron said, his gaze never wavering from the track. "One wrong move and it's over. Mika knows the plan; it's time to execute."

Across the paddock, the atmosphere in the Ferrari garage was a blend of Italian passion and meticulous preparation. Michael Schumacher, Ferrari's relentless German driver, was already suited up, his red helmet under his arm as he spoke with his engineer, Luca. "The start is crucial, but it's the long game that wins Monaco," Michael mused, his voice a calm constant amid the chaos of preparations. "We stick to the plan, stay patient, and wait for our moment."

As the race commenced, the narrow streets of Monaco became a chessboard, with each driver a moving piece in a high-speed strategic battle. Häkkinen took the lead, his McLaren slicing through the air with surgical precision, but Schumacher was never far behind, his Ferrari a constant shadow in the Finn's mirrors.

The defining moment came as the first round of pit stops approached. Tom radioed Häkkinen with a calm urgency, "Mika, we're going for the undercut. Push now, every tenth counts." In the world of Formula 1, timing and strategy during pit stops could mean the difference between victory and defeat. The undercut — a tactic where a driver pits early to take advantage of fresh tires and clear air — was a gamble in the tight and twisty Monaco circuit.

Meanwhile, Ferrari chose a different tactic for Schumacher. Luca's voice crackled over the radio, "Michael, we're staying out. Extend this stint. It's our best shot." By staying out longer before pitting, Schumacher would need to maximize his speed on older tires, a task that demanded every ounce of his skill and concentration.

The tension was palpable as Häkkinen dived into the pits, his crew ready and waiting. The pit stop was flawless, the McLaren team working as a single entity to send their driver back into the fray. Now, it was all up to Schumacher, out on the track, pushing his Ferrari to the limits of endurance and engineering.

When Schumacher finally pitted, the Ferrari team executed their stop with practiced efficiency, but as he rejoined the race, it was clear — the McLaren strategy had prevailed. Häkkinen emerged ahead, his lead solidified by the strategic gamble of his team.

The Monaco Grand Prix would end with Häkkinen taking the chequered flag, a testament not only to his skill as a driver but to the strategic acumen of the McLaren team. Schumacher and Ferrari, though beaten, were far from defeated. Their resolve only strengthened, the strategic battle in Monaco a lesson in the importance of adaptability and innovation.

As the teams packed away their equipment, the sun setting over the Mediterranean, the rivalry between McLaren and Ferrari had evolved. No longer was it just a test of speed, but a battle of minds—a game of high-speed chess where strategy, timing, and nerve played as crucial a role as the power of the engines and the courage of the drivers. This race had proven that in the quest for glory, speed, and strategy were inseparable, each as vital as the other in the pursuit of victory.

Chapter 6: Clashes and Controversies

The rivalry between McLaren and Ferrari, while built on a foundation of respect and shared passion for motorsport, was not without its moments of intense controversy and heated clashes. These incidents, played out both on the track and off, added a layer of drama to the competition, drawing fans and media into a whirlwind of speculation and debate.

The Spygate Scandal

In the mid-2000s, the world of Formula 1 found itself at the epicenter of a controversy that shook its very foundations. Dubbed "Spygate," the scandal unearthed a narrative fit for a spy novel, yet the consequences it bore were all too real for the parties involved, particularly McLaren and Ferrari. This incident wasn't just a momentary lapse; it was a saga that would indelibly alter the fabric of their rivalry and cast a long shadow over the sport's ethos of competition and fairness.

As whispers of the scandal began to permeate the paddock, the Formula 1 community found itself grappling with a maelstrom of rumors, accusations, and speculations. The revelation that confidential Ferrari documents had been found with a high-ranking McLaren engineer was a shockwave that reverberated through the circuits, from Monaco to Monza, unsettling teams, fans, and officials alike.

Within the confines of the McLaren motorhome, a palpable tension hung in the air. The team's leadership, including Ron Dennis, convened in what had become an impromptu command center, poring over the details of the accusations laid bare before them. Dennis, a figure long revered for his commitment to the integrity and honor of motorsport, found himself in the eye of the storm. "This is anathema to the values we hold dear," he stated, his voice steady yet underscored by the gravity of the situation. "Our commitment to honor and fair play defines us; we must do everything in our power to rectify this." The team, aware of the severity of the situation, nodded in agreement, understanding that the trust of their fans and the sanctity of the sport were in jeopardy.

Meanwhile, the atmosphere at Ferrari was charged with a sense of violation and disbelief. Jean Todt, the stoic team principal of Ferrari, addressed his team with a mix of calm and indignation. Standing amidst the sea of red that defined Ferrari's garage, he articulated a sentiment of profound betrayal. "Our rivalry with McLaren has always been fierce but founded on mutual respect and the shared values of our sport," Todt declared, his voice firm. "This incident not only undermines our competition but the integrity of Formula 1 as a whole. We are custodians of this sport's dignity, and such actions tarnish the legacy we strive to build."

The repercussions of the Spygate scandal were swift and unforgiving. McLaren, found in breach of possessing confidential information, faced unprecedented sanctions. The imposition of a monumental fine coupled with exclusion from the constructors' championship standings was a blow that resonated beyond the confines of the team, serving as a stark reminder of the thin line between the pursuit of a competitive edge and the imperative of ethical conduct within the sport.

The aftermath of Spygate was a period of introspection for Formula 1, prompting a reevaluation of the measures in place to safeguard the sport's integrity. For McLaren and Ferrari, the scandal was a watershed moment in their storied rivalry, a chapter that, while mired in controversy, underscored the inherent passion, commitment, and unwavering pursuit of excellence that defined both teams. As the dust settled, the incident remained a scar on the face of Formula 1, a cautionary tale of the balance between rivalry and respect, ambition and integrity.

The 2007 Championship Finale

The 2007 Formula 1 season culminated in a crescendo of anticipation and raw emotion at the Brazilian Grand Prix, the iconic Interlagos circuit setting the stage for a finale fraught with drama and tension. The air was electric, charged with the collective breath of fans worldwide, as two gladiators, McLaren's Lewis Hamilton and Ferrari's Kimi Räikkönen, prepared to etch their names in the annals of motorsport history.

Hamilton, the young prodigy from Britain, stood on the brink of an unprecedented rookie championship win. His meteoric rise through the season had been the stuff of fairytales, marked by audacious overtakes and unyielding determination. In the McLaren garage, the atmosphere was one of cautious optimism, tinged with the palpable tension of what was at stake. The engineers and mechanics, their faces etched with the season's trials, watched on, their hopes pinned on Hamilton's shoulders.

Conversely, the Ferrari camp was a blend of stoic resolve and fiery passion, emblematic of the Scuderia's storied heritage. Räikkönen, "The Iceman," was their champion—a driver whose calm demeanor belied a fierce competitor. The Finnish driver's path to the title was narrower, requiring not only a victory but also a falter from Hamilton. As the engines roared to life, Luca di Montezemolo, Ferrari's chairman, imparted a final word of encouragement to his team. "Today, we fight with the heart of a lion," he declared, his voice a rallying cry amid the roar of the crowd.

The race began with the intensity befitting a championship decider. However, early on, a twist of fate saw Hamilton's car suffer an unexpected mechanical hiccup, sending shockwaves through the McLaren team. The sight of Hamilton's car momentarily slowing was a gut punch to the team's hopes, the pit wall abuzz with frantic activity as they worked to remedy the situation. "Stay focused, Lewis. The race is long, and nothing is decided yet," came the poised encouragement from his race engineer, a beacon of hope in a moment of despair.

Meanwhile, Räikkönen, with the precision and coolness that had earned him his moniker, navigated the Interlagos circuit with a masterful command. The Ferrari pit wall was a study in focused anticipation, every lap bringing them closer to a dream that had seemed distant mere weeks ago. Di Montezemolo, watching intently, remained a picture of contained excitement, his belief in Räikkönen unwavering. "Keep your eyes on the prize, Kimi. Every corner, every lap, brings us closer," he intoned, his voice a steadying presence amidst the crescendo of engines.

As the final laps unwound and Räikkönen crossed the finish line, the Ferrari garage erupted into scenes of unbridled joy. The sea of red, a symbol of Ferrari's enduring legacy, swelled with emotion as Räikkönen clinched the championship by the slimmest of margins. It was a victory that transcended the race itself — a testament to resilience, to the belief in the face of adversity.

The 2007 Brazilian Grand Prix would be remembered not just for the drama of its race but for the profound narrative it added to the tapestry of Formula 1 — a narrative of dreams chased, of fortunes reversed, and of the razor-thin line between triumph and heartbreak. For Ferrari, it was a reaffirmation of their place at the pinnacle of motorsport; for McLaren and Hamilton, a poignant reminder of the cruelty and beauty of racing. In the end, the 2007 season finale stood as a testament to the unpredictability of Formula 1, where champions are forged in the crucible of competition, and legends are born in the heart of battle.

The Heat of the Moment

The rivalry between McLaren and Ferrari, transcending mere competition, evolved into a saga replete with high drama, embodying the essence of Formula 1's allure. This narrative was not just constructed from the high-profile scandals that shocked the world but was also woven through countless duels that played out in the heat of the moment, under the gaze of millions. Each race weekend brought with it the promise of another chapter in their storied rivalry, a testament to the unyielding pursuit of excellence that both teams epitomized.

On circuits from Monaco to Silverstone, the tension between McLaren and Ferrari was palpable, the air charged with anticipation. Each team's strategy room became a cauldron of planning and counter-planning, where every decision could lead to triumph or disaster. The rivalry was as much a battle of wits among the strategists as it was of skill among the drivers.

One memorable instance unfolded under the sweltering heat of the Italian Grand Prix at Monza, a temple of speed that has borne witness to countless tales of glory and heartbreak. In a strategic duel that had fans on the edge of their seats, McLaren attempted an audacious undercut, pitting their lead driver early in a bid to leapfrog the Ferrari ahead. The response from the Ferrari pit wall was swift, their counter-strategy executed with precision that only years of experience could afford. "Hold him off for as long as you can," came the urgent instruction over the Ferrari driver's radio, a command that would lead to a series of nail-biting laps where every corner could spell the difference between success and failure.

These moments of high tension were not confined to the strategic duels off the track but were mirrored in the daring on-track battles between the teams' drivers. Overtakes at the very limit of bravery and skill, wheel-to-wheel racing that left no room for error, and contentious incidents that sometimes saw the stewards intervene. Each incident added fuel to the fiery rivalry, sparking debates among fans and pundits alike. "Did you see that move?" became a common refrain in the stands and across social media, as replays were dissected and opinions formed.

Despite the heated moments and controversies, the enduring legacy of the McLaren-Ferrari rivalry is characterized by a mutual respect forged in the crucible of competition. It's a narrative enriched not just by their battles for supremacy but by the shared moments of sportsmanship and acknowledgment of each other's prowess. In the aftermath of contentious races, amidst the cooling down of engines and the packing up of garages, there were instances of quiet recognition between rivals, an understanding that they were all part of something much larger than themselves—a spectacle that captivated millions around the globe.

Through every disputed tactic, every controversial overtake, and every strategic duel, the McLaren-Ferrari rivalry endured as a beacon of the sport's highest values: ambition, courage, and an unwavering pursuit of excellence. These were the sparks that ignited the tinderbox of competition, ensuring that the rivalry between McLaren and Ferrari remained not just a contest of speed on the track but a compelling narrative that will be recounted for generations to come, a storied chapter in the annals of motorsport history.

Chapter 7: The Psychology of Racing

Within the high-octane world of Formula 1, where milliseconds separate triumph from defeat, the mental fortitude of drivers, engineers, and team leaders plays a pivotal role in defining success. The intense rivalry between McLaren and Ferrari served as a magnifying glass for the psychological nuances of the sport, revealing how mental resilience, team dynamics, and leadership are as crucial as the technology propelling the cars forward.

The Mind of a Champion

The psychological battlefield of Formula 1, where the world's most elite drivers converge, is as complex and nuanced as the technical war waged by engineers and designers. Within this arena, the mental fortitude of champions like Ayrton Senna of McLaren and Michael Schumacher of Ferrari stands as a testament to the mind's power over matter, their approaches emblematic of the diverse psychological landscapes navigated by those at the pinnacle of motorsport.

For Senna, the cockpit of his McLaren was a sanctum of solitude, a place where the noise of the world faded into the background, replaced by a symphony of engine notes and tire treads. In these moments, Senna transcended the physical realm of racing, entering a state of hyper-focus where time seemed to dilate, allowing him to anticipate and react with supernatural precision. This was not merely concentration; it was a meditative state, a blend of Zen and sheer willpower. "In these moments, I am not driving the car; I am the car," Senna once mused, reflecting on the symbiotic relationship he shared with his McLaren. This profound connection to his machine enabled Senna to extract performances that bordered on the miraculous, his drives in treacherous conditions becoming the stuff of legend.

Contrastingly, Michael Schumacher's dominion over his mind and his Ferrari was built on a foundation of relentless preparation and analytical precision. Schumacher approached each race as a chess master approaches the board, every move calculated, every potentiality considered. His mental rehearsals before races were exhaustive, visualizing lap after lap, corner after corner, until the circuit was etched into his memory. "To control the car, I must first control my mind," Schumacher would assert, highlighting his belief in mental preparation's paramountcy. This meticulous approach allowed Schumacher to remain unflappable under pressure, to find clarity amidst the chaos of wheel-to-wheel combat, and to execute his strategy with surgical precision.

The contrast in their psychological approaches to racing — Senna's transcendental focus versus Schumacher's calculated precision — underscores the mental diversity among champions. Yet, both methodologies share a common thread: the relentless pursuit of self-improvement and the courage to confront and conquer one's own limitations.

The quiet before the storm, the silence within the roar, represents more than just a pause before the onset of battle; it symbolizes the moment of introspection, of self-confrontation that every champion faces. Here, in the solitude of their cockpits, Senna and Schumacher engaged in the most challenging race of all — the race against the boundaries of their own potential.

As the lights go out and the world watches, the minds of these champions become arenas where battles of will, strategy, and focus unfold. It is here, in the crucible of competition, that legends are forged, and the true essence of a champion is revealed. The mind of a champion is a fortress, tempered by the fires of ambition and the relentless pursuit of excellence —

our unity. We win as a team, and we lose as a team." His words weren't mere rhetoric; they were the creed by which McLaren operated, fostering an environment where open communication flourished, and mutual respect was the foundation.

Meanwhile, within the hallowed halls of Ferrari, a different kind of alchemy took place. Here, the passionate fire that is synonymous with Italian motorsport was harnessed, forging a familial bond among the team members. Jean Todt, with his stoic demeanor and strategic mind, stood at the heart of this family. In a moment of quiet before the tempest of the race, he gathered his team, their faces a mosaic of focus and anticipation. "Our passion is the engine that drives us," Todt articulated, his voice a steady beacon amidst the storm of emotions. "But remember, it is our unity, our collective will, that makes us invincible." In his words lay the essence of Ferrari's ethos — the understanding that emotion, when channeled with precision and care, becomes a formidable force.

As the engines roared to life and the grandstands swelled with the roar of anticipation, the teams stood on the brink of another test of their mettle. The cars, technological marvels that they were, bore the hopes and dreams of their creators. But beyond the carbon fiber, beyond the meticulously tuned engines and aerodynamic contours, it was the spirit of the team that breathed life into the machine.

The grand prix unfolded, a high-speed drama under the spotlight of the global stage. The McLarens and Ferraris danced their deadly ballet at breakneck speeds, each move a testament to the countless hours of preparation and the unyielding drive of their teams. And as the checkered flag fell, marking the end of yet another chapter in their storied rivalry, it was clear that the outcome had been decided long before the cars had taken to the track. It was decided in the garages and the meeting rooms, in the hearts and minds of those who had dared to dream of victory. For in the crucible of Formula 1, where technology and talent are in constant competition, it is the unity and spirit of the team that often writes the history books.

Leadership in the Fast Lane

In the high-octane world of Formula 1, where milliseconds separate the champions from the contenders, the leadership at the helm of iconic teams like McLaren and Ferrari emerges as a pivotal force, shaping destinies with decisions made both on and off the racetrack. Ron Dennis of McLaren and the lineage of leadership at Ferrari, including the legendary Enzo Ferrari followed by Jean Todt, offered contrasting paradigms of leadership that were as distinctive in style as they were united in their effectiveness.

Ron Dennis, the architect behind McLaren's modern era of success, approached leadership with the precision of a master craftsman. His domain was one of relentless perfectionism, where every detail, no matter how minute, was scrutinized and optimized. In the sprawling McLaren Technology Centre, a manifestation of Dennis's vision, he was often seen in deep conversation with his team, his demeanor calm yet intensely focused. "The devil is in the details," Dennis would assert, his voice carrying the weight of his conviction. "Anticipate, plan, execute—this is how we stay ahead in this sport." His leadership was not just about guiding McLaren to victories; it was about instilling a culture of excellence, a relentless drive to innovate that permeated every aspect of the team's operation.

Across the divide, the corridors of Ferrari's headquarters in Maranello echoed with a different kind of ethos, one that was deeply intertwined with the passionate spirit of its founder, Enzo Ferrari, and later embodied by Jean Todt. Ferrari's leadership was visceral, rooted in the profound legacy of the Prancing Horse and the emotional connection it evoked. Enzo Ferrari, with his charismatic aura, led not just with decisions but with a vision that was as much about winning races as it was about igniting passion. "To build a great car, a winning car, you must feel it in your heart," Enzo once remarked, his words a testament to the ethos that defined Ferrari's leadership. Jean Todt, inheriting this mantle, combined strategic acumen with emotional intelligence, fostering a team environment where loyalty and passion were as critical to success as technical prowess. "Ferrari is more than a team; it's a family. And in this family, our passion fuels our pursuit of excellence," Todt would often say, capturing the essence of Ferrari's leadership philosophy.

The interplay of these contrasting leadership styles played a defining role in the storied rivalry between McLaren and Ferrari. On the track, as the engines roared and the cars blazed their trails of speed, it was the silent battles of wits, the strategies crafted in the quiet before the storm, and the cultures cultivated within each team that often tipped the scales. The meticulous planning and innovation of Dennis's

McLaren found its counterpoint in the passionate, heritage-driven approach of Ferrari's leadership.

In the crucible of Formula 1's relentless competition, the leadership of Ron Dennis and the custodians of Ferrari's legacy demonstrated that while the paths to victory may diverge, the destination remains the same. The legacy of their leadership, marked by triumphs and trials, underscores the complex tapestry of Formula 1, where technology, strategy, and emotion intertwine. It highlights the nuanced psychological battles that complement the physical contest on the track, proving that in the pursuit of glory, the mind's resilience, the unity of the team, and the vision of its leaders are the true engines of victory.

Chapter 8: Triumphs and Trophies

The rivalry between McLaren and Ferrari, two colossi striding across the Formula 1 landscape, was punctuated by moments of sheer exhilaration and crushing disappointment. Their pursuit of victory was not just about the glory of winning races but the relentless chase for the ultimate prize: the World Championship.

The Rise of McLaren: Senna's Era

The late 1980s and early 1990s heralded a transformation within the hallowed halls of McLaren, a period that would come to define the zenith of the team's storied legacy in Formula 1. Central to this era of dominance was the figure of Ayrton Senna, a driver whose name would become synonymous with the very essence of racing excellence. It was a time of intense competition, innovation, and unparalleled ambition, all encapsulated in the rivalry between Senna and his teammate, Alain Prost. This was not merely a battle for championships; it was a clash of ideologies, a duel of titans that would elevate the sport to unprecedented heights.

Senna's arrival at McLaren in 1988 was met with palpable

anticipation. From the outset, it was clear that he brought with him a fervor and dedication that was unmatched. His first championship win with McLaren in 1988 was not just a triumph; it was a declaration of his indomitable spirit and racing genius. The season itself was a canvas on which Senna painted masterstrokes of brilliance, none more so than at the Japanese Grand Prix at Suzuka.

Suzuka, with its intricate blend of high-speed corners and technical sections, was the perfect stage for what would become one of the most defining races of the era. The skies were laden with tension, the air thick with anticipation as the McLaren duo prepared for a showdown that was fraught with championship implications. Senna, starting from pole position, faced a setback that saw him drop to the back of the field. However, what followed was nothing short of miraculous.

In the McLaren garage, a symphony of emotions played out, with Ron Dennis at the helm, his gaze fixed on the monitors, watching as Senna carved his way through the field with surgical precision. Each overtaking maneuver was a testament to his relentless pursuit of victory, his McLaren MP4/4 an extension of his will. "Look at him go," Dennis whispered, a mixture of awe and anticipation in his voice. "Ayrton's driving is poetry in motion; it's as if he and the car are one."

As Senna reclaimed the lead and crossed the finish line, the McLaren garage erupted in jubilation, the tension giving way to elation. But for Dennis, this moment was more than just a victory; it was the culmination of years of perseverance, a testament to the team's dedication to excellence. "We're witnessing the emergence of not just a champion, but a legend," he remarked, his voice imbued with a sense of pride and reverence. The significance of the moment was not lost on him; under the intense pressure of championship contention, Senna had not just succeeded; he had transcended.

The rivalry between Senna and Prost, marked by both contentious battles and moments of sheer brilliance, pushed the boundaries of what was thought possible in Formula 1. Their duel was not confined to the racetracks; it extended into the very ethos of McLaren, challenging the team to innovate, to adapt, and to rise to the occasion.

In the aftermath of Suzuka, as the world celebrated Senna's triumph, the McLaren team reflected on the journey that had brought them to this pinnacle. The garages and pit walls, once the stages for strategy and competition, now stood as testaments to a golden era defined by the transcendent talent of Ayrton Senna and the visionary leadership of Ron Dennis. This period, marked by the rise of McLaren and the Senna era, would forever be etched in the annals of motorsport history, a reminder of the pursuit of excellence and the indomitable spirit of competition that defines Formula 1.

Ferrari's Resurgence: The Schumacher Years

The mid-1990s marked an era of transformation and renewed hope for Ferrari, a team with a legendary past but recent performances that had left fans yearning for more. The catalyst for this resurgence was none other than Michael Schumacher, a driver whose talent and determination were matched only by his singular quest to restore Ferrari to the pinnacle of Formula 1. Schumacher's arrival in Maranello was met with great anticipation and the weight of expectation, but it was a challenge he embraced with the same precision and focus that characterized his driving.

As the seasons progressed, the partnership between Schumacher and Ferrari began to yield results, culminating in the dramatic and emotional 2000 Formula 1 season. The

Japanese Grand Prix at Suzuka was the battlefield where years of effort, innovation, and passion converged. Schumacher's drive that day was emblematic of his entire career: calculated, relentless, and supremely skilled. Crossing the finish line, he not only secured his victory in the race but also clinched his first championship with Ferrari, ending a 21-year drought for the team in the drivers' championship.

The Ferrari garage, usually a flurry of activity, was momentarily still, the gravity of the moment sinking in. Jean Todt, the team principal, known for his stoicism, was visibly moved, the emotion evident in his eyes as he embraced his team. "This is more than a victory; it's a testament to the spirit of Ferrari," he declared, his voice steady but thick with emotion. Around him, the team erupted in a cacophony of cheers and applause, the scarlet sea of mechanics and engineers united in a moment of triumph. This victory was not just Schumacher's; it was a victory for everyone who had believed in the dream of bringing glory back to Ferrari.

The 2008 Title Decider: A Heart-Stopping Finale

Fast forward to 2008, and the Formula 1 world was again on the edge of its seat as the season reached its climax at the

Brazilian Grand Prix. In a narrative befitting the most dramatic of sporting tales, Ferrari's Felipe Massa and McLaren's Lewis Hamilton were locked in a battle for the championship, the outcome hanging in the balance until the very last moments of the race.

Massa, racing on home soil, delivered a flawless performance, leading from pole to win the race, doing everything within his power to claim the championship. As he crossed the finish line, the Brazilian crowd erupted, and for a moment, it seemed as if Massa had secured the title. In the Ferrari garage, there was a burst of joy, tempered by the tense wait for Hamilton's final position.

Meanwhile, in the McLaren garage, the tension was palpable. Hamilton, needing to finish fifth to secure the championship, found himself in sixth place as the race neared its conclusion. However, in a twist that could only happen in Formula 1, he managed to overtake Timo Glock in the final corners of the race, securing the necessary position to win the championship by a single point.

The contrasting emotions in the McLaren and Ferrari garages were a stark illustration of the fine line between triumph and heartbreak in Formula 1. While McLaren celebrated, the mood in the Ferrari camp was one of disbelief and disappointment. "That was the longest lap of my life," Hamilton later confessed, the enormity of what he had achieved finally dawning on him. For Massa, despite the heartbreak of losing the championship, his gracious demeanor in defeat and his victory in front of his home crowd solidified his status as a hero in the hearts of fans.

These moments, rich in drama and emotion, are emblematic of the highs and lows that define Formula 1. They underscore not just the technical and physical challenges of the sport but also the psychological resilience and sheer will required to compete at the highest level. The stories of Ferrari's resurgence and the heart-stopping finale of the 2008 season are chapters in the annals of motorsport history, testaments to the enduring spirit of competition and the relentless pursuit of excellence that drives teams like Ferrari and McLaren.

The Legacy of Rivalry

Spanning the echelons of time, the rivalry between McLaren and Ferrari has woven a rich tapestry within the realm of Formula 1, a narrative punctuated by epic battles, monumental triumphs, and poignant defeats. It is a saga that has not only defined careers but also shaped the very foundation of the sport, pushing its boundaries and setting new paradigms of excellence.

As the engines roar to life and the lights go out, signaling the start of yet another chapter in their storied contest, it's the collective spirit of the teams—drivers, engineers, strategists, and mechanics—each playing a critical role, that crafts the legend. From the drawing boards and simulators to the pit lanes and podiums, every victory carved by McLaren and every triumph claimed by Ferrari added depth to their rivalry, imbuing it with a significance that transcends the confines of the racetrack.

In the aftermath of each race, the air within the McLaren and Ferrari garages was thick with a myriad of emotions. Victories were celebrated with fervor, a testament to the relentless pursuit and the sacrifices made in the quest for supremacy. Yet, in moments of defeat, the atmosphere was reflective, marked by a solemn vow to emerge stronger, to learn from the lessons etched in the heat of battle. It was within these moments that the true essence of the rivalry revealed itself—

not just as a contest of speed and strategy but as an enduring commitment to excellence and innovation.

Beyond the fierce competition, a profound sense of mutual respect was forged between McLaren and Ferrari, an acknowledgment of the shared journey, of the trials and triumphs that each faced in the pursuit of glory. This respect was mirrored in the exchanges between team principals, the sportsmanlike gestures of drivers on the podium, and the gracious acknowledgments in times of victory and defeat. It underscored a recognition that their rivalry, while fierce, was a catalyst that propelled Formula 1 to new heights, captivating fans around the globe and inspiring aspiring racers dreaming of one day taking their place among the legends.

The legacy of the McLaren-Ferrari rivalry is etched not only in the silverware and the records but in the indomitable spirit it fostered, a testament to the relentless pursuit of perfection. It is a legacy that transcends generations, engaging fans in a narrative rich with heroism, heartbreak, and the undying quest for excellence. The trophies and titles, symbols of their achievements, are but milestones along a journey that continues to shape the destiny of Formula 1.

As the sun sets on each grand prix, casting long shadows across the tarmac, the legacy of the McLaren-Ferrari rivalry lingers in the air, a reminder of the battles waged and the history forged on the world's greatest racing stages. It is a legacy that continues to inspire, a beacon for the future generations of racers, engineers, and fans alike, a poignant reminder that at the heart of Formula 1 lies not just a sport, but a celebration of human endeavor, a pursuit of excellence that knows no bounds.

Chapter 9: Innovations and Accusations

In the high-stakes world of Formula 1, where technological superiority can be the difference between victory and defeat, the pursuit of innovation is relentless. This quest, while driving the sport forward, has also been the source of some of its most contentious episodes. The rivalry between McLaren and Ferrari, emblematic of Formula 1's competitive spirit, has not been immune to controversies surrounding innovations and accusations, particularly those of espionage and legal battles that have left an indelible mark on the sport.

The Espionage Saga

The mid-2000s were a tumultuous period for Formula 1, marked by an espionage scandal that sent shockwaves through the paddock. At the heart of the controversy were allegations that confidential technical information from Ferrari had found its way into the hands of McLaren personnel. The saga unfolded like a spy thriller, complete with clandestine meetings, secret communications, and a dossier of documents that threatened to unravel the fabric of trust that held the sport together.

The impact was immediate and profound. McLaren faced severe sanctions, including a record fine and disqualification from the constructors' championship. The controversy dominated headlines, overshadowing the on-track battles and casting a shadow over the sport's integrity. "This is a regrettable chapter in the annals of Formula 1," lamented Ron Dennis, grappling with the fallout that threatened to tarnish McLaren's legacy.

Ferrari, for its part, was vindicated in its pursuit of justice but bemoaned the circumstances that led to such a breach of trust. "We compete to be the best, but integrity must be the cornerstone of our sport," reflected Jean Todt, embodying the sense of betrayal felt by the Scuderia.

Legal Battles and Their Repercussions

In the high-stakes arena of Formula 1, where the quest for supremacy pushes teams to the zenith of technological innovation, McLaren and Ferrari found themselves embroiled in legal battles that tested the limits of competition and camaraderie. The espionage scandal, while most prominent, was merely the tip of the iceberg in a series of legal entanglements that spanned disputes over intellectual property, allegations of poaching personnel, and accusations of rule-breaking. These skirmishes, played out in the stark, cold rooms of legal arbitration, highlighted the razor-thin margin between leading the pack and crossing the bounds of fair play.

In one such episode, the paddock was rife with whispers of a key engineer moving from Maranello to Woking, bringing with him a treasure trove of knowledge and secrets. "It's not just about the individual," remarked a senior Ferrari executive during a tense, closed-door meeting with their McLaren counterparts, the air thick with accusation and defense. "It's about the integrity of the sport. We're here to compete, yes, but not at the cost of honor."

Across the table, a McLaren representative, calm yet firm, responded, "Our goal has always been to innovate, to push the boundaries. Yes, we welcome talent, but we do so with respect for the rules that bind us all. Let's not forget, we're all guardians of this sport's legacy."

The resolution of these disputes often remained shrouded in confidentiality, the details known only to those who navigated these stormy waters. Yet, the repercussions echoed far beyond the boardrooms and courtrooms. They catalyzed a shift within Formula 1, prompting the governing bodies to tighten the reins on the transfer of technology and personnel. "We find ourselves at a crossroads," announced the FIA president in a landmark address to the teams and media, the seriousness of the moment reflected in his measured tone. "The fabric of our sport is woven with the spirit of competition, but let us not fray it with the scissors of deceit. The path of innovation must walk hand in hand with integrity."

This proclamation marked a new era in Formula 1, one where surveillance and scrutiny became as much a part of the game as aerodynamics and horsepower. The introduction of new regulations aimed at safeguarding the sport's integrity was met with mixed reactions. In a candid moment, reflecting on the changes, a veteran engineer mused, "We've always danced on the edge of what's possible, but now, the dance floor has boundaries. It's a new challenge, but perhaps it's what we need to keep the essence of this sport pure."

The legacy of these legal battles, while marred by contention, ultimately served to reinforce the foundation of Formula 1 on principles of fair play and ethical competition. The rivalries on the track continued, as fierce as ever, but underscored by a renewed commitment to respect the rules of engagement. "What we've gone through," reflected a team principal, "has not only tested our resolve but reaffirmed our dedication to the sport we love. We race not just for glory, but for the honor of competition."

In the grand tapestry of Formula 1's history, the legal skirmishes between McLaren and Ferrari added complex shades to the rivalry, reminding all involved that the pursuit of excellence demands not just innovation and speed but a steadfast adherence to the principles that define the spirit of fair competition.

The Impact on the Sport

The espionage saga and subsequent legal battles that unfolded between McLaren and Ferrari did not just mark chapters of contention in the annals of Formula 1 history; they catalyzed a transformative shift within the sport. In the wake of these events, Formula 1 found itself at a crossroads, navigating the delicate balance between the relentless pursuit of technological edge and the imperative of maintaining ethical standards. The aftermath of these controversies ushered in an era of increased regulation, transparency, and a concerted emphasis on ethical conduct, reshaping the landscape of Formula 1.

The governing bodies, spurred by the need to safeguard the sport's integrity, implemented a series of stringent regulations aimed at preventing the recurrence of such incidents. The paddock, once a secretive enclave where teams guarded their innovations with zeal, was now a realm of increased scrutiny. "We've entered a new era of transparency," announced the FIA president in a landmark address, his words resonating across the teams and fans alike. "The spirit of competition must be underpinned by fairness and respect. These are the pillars upon which our sport shall stand."

This shift was met with mixed reactions. Some mourned the loss of the 'wild west' days of technological espionage, while others welcomed the change, viewing it as necessary for the sport's long-term sustainability. Amidst this evolution, the rivalry between McLaren and Ferrari, rather than waning, found new ground. The adversities and legal skirmishes, instead of driving a wedge between the teams, fostered a deeper mutual respect. "The challenges we've faced, the battles we've fought, have not divided us; they've united us in our love for this sport," reflected a senior Ferrari engineer, his words echoing the sentiments of many within the paddock.

This newfound respect was not limited to the corridors of power within the teams but extended to the fans and stakeholders. The controversies sparked widespread debates about the nature of competition and innovation in Formula 1, engaging the community in a discourse about the ethical boundaries of technological advancement. "Where do we draw the line?" became a recurring question in forums, social media, and among the fandom, reflecting a collective introspection about the values that define the sport.

In the grand tapestry of Formula 1, the episodes of espionage and legal wrangling between McLaren and Ferrari are more than mere footnotes; they are pivotal moments that prompted a reevaluation of the sport's guiding principles. The resultant era of regulation and ethical emphasis did not stifle the spirit of innovation but rather channeled it within a framework of integrity and fairness.

As Formula 1 continues to evolve, pushing the limits of what is technologically possible while navigating the complexities of competition, the legacy of these episodes serves as a reminder of the sport's resilience. It underscores the capacity of Formula 1 to adapt, to emerge stronger and more united in the face of challenges, steadfastly upholding the principles of respect and integrity that are the hallmarks of motorsport excellence. The rivalry between McLaren and Ferrari, enriched by this chapter of their history, continues to captivate, a testament to their unyielding passion for racing and a symbol of the enduring spirit that drives Formula 1 forward.

Chapter 10: Legends Behind the Wheel

In the grand theater of Formula 1, where engineering marvels meet the crucible of competition, it's the drivers who become the face of the sport's triumphs, tragedies, and tales of sheer will. The rivalry between McLaren and Ferrari has been graced by some of the most iconic figures in racing history — drivers whose skill, bravery, and charisma transcended the cockpit and left an indelible mark on the hearts of fans worldwide.

Ayrton Senna: The Soul of McLaren

The era of Ayrton Senna at McLaren transcends mere statistics and championship titles; it represents a chapter where the soul of racing was epitomized by one man's relentless pursuit of excellence. Senna's integration into McLaren in 1988 wasn't just a signing; it was the fusion of a driver's fierce determination with a team's innovative spirit, heralding the start of what many consider the golden era of Formula 1.

Senna brought to McLaren a level of intensity and focus that was unparalleled. His interactions with the team, from mechanics to engineers, infused McLaren with a new ethos.

"When Ayrton spoke about the car, we all listened," recalled a McLaren engineer, "It was as if he could feel the car's soul." This deep connection wasn't confined to the spiritual; it had tangible impacts on the car's development. Senna's feedback, born from his acute sensitivity to the car's behavior, led to innovations that pushed the boundaries of what was technically conceivable.

The rivalry with Prost, both as a teammate and adversary, is often cited not just for its competitive ferocity but for the way it drove both drivers to new heights. In the confines of the McLaren garage, the air was thick with a competitive tension that was palpable, yet it was underpinned by a mutual respect for each other's skill and dedication. "Their battles were intense," a team strategist remarked, "but it was that intensity that drove us forward. They demanded the best from themselves, from us, from the car."

Nowhere was Senna's extraordinary talent more visible than at the rain-soaked 1988 Japanese Grand Prix at Suzuka. From the back of the field, Senna weaved a narrative of resilience and audacity, staging a comeback that is etched in the annals of motorsport lore. Ron Dennis, from his vantage point on the pit wall, watched as Senna not just raced but transcended the limits of possibility. "Ayrton is not just driving; he's composing a symphony," Dennis remarked, encapsulating the ethereal connection between driver and machine that defined Senna's era at McLaren.

Senna's impact on McLaren extended beyond the cockpit. He shaped the culture of the team, instilling a drive for perfection that permeated every aspect of their operation. "He elevated us," said a long-serving team member, "His legacy is not just in the trophies and the victories; it's in the relentless pursuit of excellence that became our creed."

Reflecting on Senna's legacy, it's clear that his influence reverberates far beyond his years at McLaren. New generations of drivers, engineers, and fans draw inspiration from his dedication, his spirit, and his unwavering commitment to the art of racing. "Every time we face a challenge, we ask ourselves, what would Ayrton do?" shares a young McLaren driver, a testament to the enduring legacy of Senna's time with the team.

Senna's era at McLaren, marked by breathtaking victories, heart-wrenching challenges, and an insatiable quest for perfection, remains a defining chapter in Formula 1 history.

It's a narrative that transcends the sport, a reminder of the power of passion, the importance of innovation, and the indomitable spirit of competition. In the story of McLaren, and indeed in the history of Formula 1, Ayrton Senna stands as a towering figure, a driver whose quest for perfection sought not just to redefine the limits of racing but to capture the very soul of it.

Michael Schumacher: The Red Baron of Ferrari

Michael Schumacher's arrival at Ferrari in the mid-1990s signified more than just a change of teams; it marked the beginning of a transformative journey for both the driver and the iconic Italian marque. His integration into Ferrari was akin to the infusion of a vital force that would reinvigorate the team's aspirations and set them on a path to unparalleled success.

Schumacher's approach to racing was holistic. He didn't just drive; he immersed himself in every aspect of the team's operation, from the nuances of car development to the strategies deployed on race day. His collaboration with the engineers was symbiotic, pushing the boundaries of innovation and car performance. "We've found a new gear with Michael," a senior engineer at Ferrari remarked. "His input is invaluable; he sees the potential in every detail."

This meticulous dedication was mirrored in Schumacher's preparation. He was known for his exhaustive physical training regimen, which ensured that he was as sharp in the final laps of a race as he was in the first. But beyond the physical, Schumacher's mental resilience stood out. Facing challenges, whether in the form of on-track rivals or the intense pressure of expectations, he remained unflappable, his focus unwavering.

The crowning moment of Schumacher's relentless pursuit came at the 2000 Japanese Grand Prix at Suzuka. The race was a crucible, testing not just the speed of the car but the spirit of the team. Schumacher's victory, securing his first championship with Ferrari, was a cathartic release for the entire Scuderia. The jubilation in the Ferrari garage was palpable, a mixture of relief and vindication, as years of effort finally culminated in triumph.

Jean Todt, usually reserved, couldn't hide his emotions. Standing amidst the celebration, he reflected on Schumacher's impact: "Michael has redefined what it means to be a part of

Ferrari. He's not just a driver; he's the essence, the very heart that drives us to victory. Today, we're not just celebrating a championship; we're celebrating the rebirth of Ferrari's racing spirit."

In the years that followed, Schumacher's influence on Ferrari transcended his contributions on the track. He became a mentor, a guiding figure for younger drivers, and an integral part of the Ferrari family. His legacy was not merely the titles and trophies but the culture of excellence and determination he instilled in the team.

As Schumacher's era at Ferrari is reminisced, it's clear that his legacy is woven into the fabric of the Scuderia. The period of dominance, the relentless pursuit of victory, and the resurrection of Ferrari's fortunes in Formula 1 are all chapters in the storied history of the sport, chapters that bear the indelible mark of Michael Schumacher's drive, determination, and spirit. His time at Ferrari is remembered not just for the victories and championships but for the resurgence of a team that, under his influence, re-established itself as a titan of motorsport.

Lewis Hamilton: The Prodigy of McLaren

When Lewis Hamilton made his Formula 1 debut with McLaren in 2007, the motorsport world watched with bated breath as a prodigy took to the stage. With a blend of raw speed and a fearless racing style, Hamilton was not just a rookie; he was a herald of a new era in Formula 1. His maiden season was nothing short of spectacular, challenging seasoned veterans and defying expectations at every turn. The culmination of this remarkable entry into the world of Formula 1 was the Brazilian Grand Prix, a race that would etch Hamilton's name in the annals of the sport's history, not for the victory he narrowly missed but for the promise of greatness it foretold.

The McLaren garage during that fateful race in Brazil was a crucible of tension and anticipation. The team, fully aware of Hamilton's prodigious talent, watched as the championship slipped through their fingers in the final moments, a heartbreak that was palpable in the air. Yet, amidst the disappointment, there was a sense of inevitable triumph. "We've seen what Lewis is capable of," remarked a senior McLaren engineer, his eyes reflecting a mix of pride and resolve. "This isn't the end; it's just the start of a journey that will take us to heights we've only dreamed of."

Hamilton's response to the setback was characteristic of the champion he was destined to become. With determination etched on his face, he looked beyond the disappointment, seeing not a defeat but a stepping stone. "This is just the beginning," Hamilton stated with conviction, his eyes alight with the fire of unfulfilled ambition. "We'll come back stronger, faster, and more determined. The best is yet to come."

True to his word, Hamilton's journey with McLaren saw him ascend to the pinnacle of Formula 1 the following year. The 2008 season was a testament to his resilience, his capacity to learn from every race, every lap, every corner. The Brazilian Grand Prix that year was again the stage for a dramatic finale, but this time, fate smiled on Hamilton. In a moment that has since become legend, Hamilton secured his first World Championship title in the dying moments of the race, a victory that was as much about his fighting spirit as it was about his unparalleled skill behind the wheel.

The celebrations that erupted in the McLaren garage were a release of pent-up emotions, a mix of joy, relief, and vindication. Ron Dennis, the mastermind behind McLaren's success, watched with a sense of paternal pride as Hamilton climbed out of his car, the world champion at last. "What Lewis has achieved is extraordinary," Dennis commented, the significance of the moment not lost on him. "He's not just won a championship; he's inspired a generation. This is a victory for every one of us who believes in the power of dreams."

Hamilton's story with McLaren, from his sensational debut to his dramatic championship win, is more than a tale of victories and defeats. It's a narrative that captures the essence of Formula 1 racing: the relentless pursuit of excellence, the courage to face adversity, and the indomitable will to emerge victorious. Hamilton's legacy at McLaren is not merely measured in trophies and titles but in the indelible mark he left on the team and the sport, a legacy that continues to inspire and captivate fans around the world.

Fernando Alonso: The Fighter in Red and Silver

Fernando Alonso's journey through the echelons of Formula 1 is a testament to his indomitable spirit and tactical acumen, characteristics that he carried with him whether adorned in the scarlet of Ferrari or the silver and red of McLaren. Alonso, a driver who seamlessly blended raw speed with cerebral strategy, reshaped the contours of modern racing, challenging his peers and the sport itself to rise to his level.

With McLaren, Alonso brought a relentless drive and an insatiable hunger for victory. His arrival at the team was heralded with great anticipation, for here was a driver who had already tasted the pinnacle of success and yet yearned for more. The McLaren garage, accustomed to the pursuit of excellence, found in Alonso a kindred spirit. "Fernando doesn't just want to win; he needs to win," remarked a McLaren engineer, highlighting the depth of Alonso's competitive nature.

His tenure with Ferrari, meanwhile, was characterized by moments that underscored his brilliance behind the wheel and his capacity to inspire those around him. The Ferrari team, with its rich history and passionate fanbase, embraced Alonso not just as a driver but as a symbol of their aspirations. In the heat of competition, Alonso's resolve became a beacon for the team, driving them forward. "Fernando wears his heart on his sleeve," observed a Ferrari strategist. "His passion for racing mirrors our own. It's what makes him not just a driver, but a Ferrari driver."

The 2007 European Grand Prix at the Nürburgring stands as a shining example of Alonso's exceptional skill and determination. In a race marred by capricious weather, Alonso's mastery of the elements and the circuit propelled him to a stunning victory, a triumph that was about more than just tactical brilliance — it was a victory of will. As the rain lashed down, turning the track into a treacherous labyrinth of standing water and slick asphalt, Alonso remained unfazed, his focus unyielding.

In the aftermath of the race, as the paddock buzzed with the excitement of his victory, Alonso reflected on what drove him to push the limits of possibility. "Racing is in my blood," he stated, the emotion evident in his voice. "It's more than just a sport to me; it's a calling. Every time I'm behind the wheel, I'm not just racing against others; I'm challenging myself, striving to be better, to be the best."

Alonso's journey with McLaren and Ferrari, marked by breathtaking highs and challenging lows, was not just a chronicle of his quest for championships; it was a narrative that highlighted his role as a catalyst for change. In Alonso, the sport found not just a formidable competitor but a driver who could elevate the teams he was a part of, pushing them to innovate, to adapt, and to overcome.

As the sun sets on each race weekend, the legacy of Fernando Alonso remains etched in the memories of fans and the history of Formula 1. His time in red and silver was more than a series of races; it was a saga of resilience, of battles fought with indomitable spirit and a relentless pursuit of greatness. Alonso's story with McLaren and Ferrari is a vivid chapter in the annals of motorsport, a testament to the enduring allure of racing and the unquenchable thirst for victory that defines champions.

These legends behind the wheel, each with their unique style, personality, and approach to racing, have been pivotal in defining the McLaren-Ferrari rivalry. Their contributions went beyond the cockpit, influencing team strategies, car development, and the broader narrative of Formula 1. They were not just competitors; they were storytellers, each lap and each race adding to the lore of the sport. The legacy of their rivalries, triumphs, and trials continues to inspire new generations of drivers and fans alike, a testament to the enduring allure of Formula 1's quest for speed, excellence, and glory.

Chapter 11: The New Era

As the 21st century unfolded, the Formula 1 landscape began to shift. New technologies, sweeping regulatory changes, and the emergence of fresh talent heralded a new era for the sport and for the enduring rivalry between McLaren and Ferrari. This chapter explores how these factors influenced the competition between the two storied teams, adapting to the evolving challenges and opportunities that shaped the modern face of Formula 1.

The Hybrid Revolution

The dawn of the hybrid era in Formula 1 represented not just a regulatory change but a revolution in the very essence of motor racing technology. In 2014, the introduction of hybrid power units transformed the sport, intertwining the raw, unbridled power of traditional combustion engines with the silent, instantaneous force of electric motors and sophisticated energy recovery systems. This paradigm shift towards sustainability and efficiency was not without its challenges, but it provided a unique canvas for teams like McLaren and Ferrari, bastions of innovation, to illustrate their engineering prowess and commitment to the future of motorsport.

McLaren, a team with a storied history of pushing the boundaries of technology, embarked on a partnership with Honda that was emblematic of their pioneering spirit. This alliance was driven by a shared vision to lead Formula 1 into a new era, leveraging Honda's expertise in hybrid technology. However, the path to integration was strewn with obstacles, each one a testament to the complex dance of maximizing performance within the confines of the new regulations. In the McLaren technology center, a hive of activity buzzed with the energy of engineers and designers working tirelessly to marry the powertrain's components into a cohesive unit. "We're venturing into uncharted territory," the team principal remarked during a strategy meeting, his voice steady but tinged with the weight of expectation. "But it's in our DNA to innovate, to overcome. We are, and always will be, pioneers on the frontier of racing technology."

Meanwhile, at Ferrari's Maranello base, the transition into the hybrid era was met with a characteristic blend of passion and precision. The team's engineers, drawing upon decades of experience in pushing the limits of automotive engineering, approached the challenge with a mix of reverence for the brand's heritage and an unyielding drive to innovate. The development of Ferrari's hybrid power unit was a marvel of engineering, a powerhouse of efficiency and performance that maintained the soul-stirring sound and ferocity for which Ferrari was renowned. "In this new era, our objective remains the same: to win," Ferrari's lead engineer mused, overlooking the dynamometer tests of the new power unit. "But we do so by forging a deeper connection between driver, machine, and the environment. It's about achieving harmony, where every component, every system, works in concert."

The Hybrid Revolution brought with it a renaissance of sorts in Formula 1, challenging teams to rethink strategies, to innovate not just for the sake of competition but for the future of the automotive industry. The journey of McLaren and Ferrari through this era was emblematic of the sport's resilience, its ability to adapt and evolve. As the engines roared to life, echoing the synthesis of tradition and technology, it was clear that Formula 1 was on the cusp of a new chapter, one that would be written by the hands of those daring enough to embrace change and steer the course of history.

In the grand tapestry of Formula 1, the Hybrid Revolution marked a pivotal moment, a confluence of competition, innovation, and stewardship for the planet. For McLaren and Ferrari, it was an opportunity to once again assert their dominance, not just as competitors but as vanguards of a future where speed and sustainability are not mutually exclusive but are instead intertwined in the quest for racing excellence.

Navigating Regulatory Changes

The ever-evolving landscape of Formula 1 regulations has continually pushed teams to adapt, innovate, and sometimes, reinvent their strategies to remain at the pinnacle of motorsport. Both McLaren and Ferrari, with their storied histories and deep-rooted commitment to excellence, have been instrumental in navigating these changes, influencing the direction of the sport while remaining steadfast competitors on the track.

The introduction of budget caps and aerodynamic testing restrictions marked a watershed moment for Formula 1, heralding a new era where the emphasis on financial prudence and technical ingenuity became paramount. For teams accustomed to operating at the zenith of technological advancement, these changes presented a unique set of challenges and opportunities.

At McLaren, the response to these regulatory shifts was characterized by a blend of strategic foresight and adaptability. "We're entering uncharted waters," acknowledged McLaren's strategy chief during a team briefing, the room filled with the team's top engineers and strategists. "But within every challenge lies an opportunity. The budget caps and testing restrictions are designed to level the playing field, which means our approach to innovation and development needs to be smarter, more efficient. We need to think not just about how much we spend, but how we spend it."

The sentiment was echoed at Ferrari, where the legacy of success and the pressure to maintain their status as frontrunners in the sport weighed heavily. "These changes are a test of our ingenuity, our passion," Ferrari's lead engineer reflected during a discussion with his team. The walls of the Ferrari meeting room, adorned with images of historic victories and legendary drivers, served as a poignant reminder of the team's heritage and the expectations that came with it. "We have always prided ourselves on being at the forefront of innovation. The introduction of budget caps and testing restrictions doesn't change that; it simply sets new boundaries within which we must work. Our task is to continue pushing the limits, to find new ways to extract performance and efficiency from every euro spent, from every second in the wind tunnel."

The dialogue between the teams and the sport's governing body was ongoing, with both McLaren and Ferrari actively participating in discussions to shape the future of Formula 1 regulations. Their contributions were not just about safeguarding their interests but were reflective of a broader commitment to the health and sustainability of the sport. "It's imperative that we find a balance," stated a high-ranking official from the FIA during a regulatory summit. "The expertise and input of teams like McLaren and Ferrari are invaluable as we navigate these changes. Together, we're working towards a future where Formula 1 remains the pinnacle of motor racing, both in terms of competition and innovation."

As the sport continues to evolve, the role of McLaren and Ferrari in navigating and shaping regulatory changes remains critical. Their ability to adapt, to innovate within the confines of new rules, and to maintain the essence of competition that defines Formula 1 is a testament to their legacy and a beacon for the future of the sport. In the quest for speed, safety, and sustainability, the journey of McLaren and Ferrari through the maze of regulatory evolution is a compelling narrative of resilience, ingenuity, and an unyielding pursuit of excellence..

The Arrival of New Faces

In the grand theatre of Formula 1, where legends are etched into the annals of history through sheer velocity and unyielding will, the arrival of Charles Leclerc at Ferrari and Lando Norris at McLaren signaled the dawn of a new era. These young titans, with their remarkable talent and infectious passion, have reinvigorated the age-old rivalry between the two storied teams, promising a future as thrilling as the chapters that preceded them.

Charles Leclerc, with his piercing gaze and a demeanor that belies a fierce competitive spirit, has quickly ascended as the beacon of Ferrari's resurgence. His performances on the track, characterized by a mesmerizing blend of raw speed and an uncanny ability to outthink his opponents, have drawn comparisons to the greats who have donned the scarlet suit before him. Leclerc's meteoric rise within the team is not just a testament to his driving prowess but also to his profound connection with the essence of Ferrari. "Racing for Ferrari is not just about the speed or the victories," Leclerc mused, a slight smile playing on his lips as he reflected on his journey. "It's about being part of a legacy, about racing for every kid who dreams of this seat. It's an honor and a responsibility I don't take lightly."

Meanwhile, Lando Norris, with his boyish charm and an easy smile that often disguises the steely resolve of a seasoned racer, has become the embodiment of McLaren's ambitious stride towards reclaiming its former glory. Norris, whose talent behind the wheel is matched by his savvy use of strategy and his innate ability to connect with fans off the track, has quickly become a fan favorite and a cornerstone of McLaren's future. "To drive fast is one thing," Norris said, his eyes lighting up with the sheer joy of racing. "But to push a team forward, to be part of its journey back to the top, that's what drives me every day."

The rivalry, enriched by the emergence of these formidable talents, is set for a seismic shift with the announcement that Lewis Hamilton, a name synonymous with speed, determination, and an unparalleled record of success, will join

Ferrari in 2025. Hamilton's move to the Scuderia is not just a transfer; it's a historic moment that promises to redefine the contours of Formula 1's competitive landscape. "Joining Ferrari is a new chapter, a new challenge," Hamilton declared, his voice imbued with anticipation and a hint of reverence for the team's storied history. "It's about testing my limits, about bringing everything I've learned to the table. We share a common goal—to win, to create history. And I can't wait to get started."

The anticipation surrounding Hamilton's arrival at Ferrari, coupled with the burgeoning talents of Leclerc and Norris, heralds a thrilling new chapter in the annals of Formula 1. As these drivers, each with their unique blend of skill, charisma, and competitive zeal, prepare to face off on the world's grandest racing stages, they carry with them the legacy of their teams and the promise of epic battles to come. The rivalry between McLaren and Ferrari, enriched by new faces and renewed ambitions, continues to be a testament to the enduring allure of Formula 1—a saga of speed, strategy, and the unyielding pursuit of excellence that captivates fans around the globe.

The rivalry between McLaren and Ferrari, enriched by new

technologies, regulatory landscapes, and emerging talent, continues to evolve. It's a testament to the enduring spirit of competition that defines Formula 1, a sport perpetually on the cutting edge of innovation, where history and future converge on the racetrack, propelling the legacy of two of its greatest teams into the new era.

Chapter 12: Beyond the Track

The rivalry between McLaren and Ferrari, a saga woven into the very fabric of Formula 1, transcends the confines of race tracks and the roar of engines. Its impact resonates beyond the paddock, influencing automotive engineering, shaping the culture of motorsport, and captivating the imaginations of fans worldwide. This chapter delves into how the storied competition between these two titans has left an indelible mark on the world beyond Formula 1.

Innovations that Drive the Future

As the horizon of Formula 1 extends into the future, the technological arms race between titans McLaren and Ferrari continues to blaze trails, not just on the racetracks but across the broader spectrum of automotive engineering. Their relentless pursuit of supremacy has been a crucible for innovation, where advancements in aerodynamics, materials science, and powertrain technologies have not only redefined the parameters of racing but have also heralded a new epoch in the consumer automotive market.

McLaren, with its pioneering spirit, has delved into the realms of carbon fiber composites, transforming the landscape of chassis construction. This foray into lightweight materials has not been confined to the pursuit of milliseconds on the track; it has opened up vistas of possibilities for the automotive industry at large. "The challenges we face on the track push us towards solutions that have the power to change the automotive world," observed a McLaren engineer, reflecting on the broader implications of their work. "Our exploration of carbon fiber composites is a perfect example. What started as a quest for competitive advantage in Formula 1 is now revolutionizing how cars are built, making them not just faster but safer and more efficient."

Ferrari's contributions to this technological odyssey have been equally transformative. The Scuderia's mastery over engine performance and hybrid technologies has not only secured its place in the pantheon of racing legends but has also paved the way for groundbreaking developments in high-performance road vehicles. The expertise honed on the circuit—balancing raw power with efficiency—finds a parallel expression in Ferrari's line of road cars. A Ferrari designer, contemplating the seamless flow of innovation from track to road, shared, "Our successes in racing, each lap, each victory, are distilled into lessons that shape the future of our road cars. It's a testament to Enzo Ferrari's vision of synergy between our racing endeavors and our automotive creations."

Looking ahead, the landscape of Formula 1 and the automotive industry is poised for further evolution, driven by the advancements spearheaded by McLaren and Ferrari. As the world pivots towards sustainability, the research into alternative fuels, energy recovery systems, and advanced aerodynamics by these teams is setting the stage for a future where high performance and environmental stewardship go hand in hand. "The next frontier is not just speed; it's sustainability," a team strategist from Ferrari mused, hinting at the shifting focus of future innovations.

In this context, the rivalry between McLaren and Ferrari transcends the confines of competition; it becomes a catalyst for progress, pushing the envelope of what's possible both on the track and on the road. As these teams continue to innovate in the crucible of Formula 1, their legacy is not only etched in trophies and record books but also in the advancements that shape the future of mobility. "We're racing towards a future where every vehicle benefits from the lessons learned at 300 kilometers per hour," a McLaren engineer concluded, encapsulating the essence of their journey. The path charted by McLaren and Ferrari is a testament to the enduring impact of their rivalry, a legacy that extends far beyond the checkered flags to redefine the future of the automotive world.

Cultivating Motorsport Culture

The tapestry of Formula 1, woven with the threads of speed, innovation, and fierce competition, finds its richest colors in the rivalry between McLaren and Ferrari. This historic contest has not only defined epochs within the sport but has also significantly influenced the culture of motorsport, etching itself into the hearts and minds of fans and enthusiasts worldwide. The battles waged on the world's most illustrious tracks have become the stuff of legend, narratives imbued with the essence of human endeavor that continue to inspire and captivate.

The impact of the McLaren-Ferrari rivalry on the global motorsport culture is profound, transcending the confines of the racetrack to kindle a passion for racing in the hearts of countless individuals. From the engineering marvels that grace the circuit to the strategic duels that unfold in the pit lanes, every facet of their contest speaks to the ingenuity and resilience that are the hallmarks of Formula 1. "Every race is a story, a lesson in what it means to push the limits," shared a veteran journalist at a fan gathering, his words resonating with an audience hanging on to every recounted tale of McLaren and Ferrari's duels.

The influence of these storied teams has ignited a fervor for motorsport that spans the globe, inspiring many to not just follow the sport but to become an active part of it. Young enthusiasts, inspired by the exploits of their heroes on the track, embark on careers in engineering, hoping to contribute to the next breakthrough in racing technology. Aspiring drivers, their walls adorned with posters of McLaren and Ferrari's legendary machines, dream of the day they might steer such marvels themselves. "It's more than just a fascination; it's a calling," confided a young engineer at a university motorsport club meeting, his aspirations a testament to the impact of the rivalry's legacy.

Beyond the technical and competitive aspects, the McLaren-Ferrari rivalry has fostered a rich community culture, binding fans in a shared passion that often transcends geographic and cultural boundaries. Motorsport clubs, online forums, and fan events buzz with spirited debates and discussions, each chapter of the rivalry dissected and celebrated. These platforms have become crucibles of camaraderie, where tales of triumph and heartbreak are shared, fostering a sense of belonging among fans. "This rivalry, it's what makes Formula 1 so compelling," noted a fan during an online forum discussion, capturing the sentiment of a community united by their shared passion for the sport.

The legacy of the McLaren-Ferrari rivalry in cultivating motorsport culture is indelible. It has not only elevated the sport but has also sown the seeds of passion and aspiration in the hearts of those who follow it. The stories of triumph, controversy, and human spirit that emanate from their contest enrich the narrative of Formula 1, serving as a beacon for future generations. As the engines roar and the rivalry unfolds with each passing season, McLaren and Ferrari continue to shape not just the future of racing but also the culture that surrounds it, ensuring that motorsport remains a vibrant and integral part of the global sporting landscape.

Bridging Communities and Inspiring Dreams

The storied rivalry between McLaren and Ferrari transcends the confines of the racetrack, casting a far-reaching shadow that touches not only the realm of motorsport but also the broader fabric of society. This legendary contest, steeped in a history of technological innovation and cultural impact, stands as a monument to the aspirational values of dedication, excellence, and the unyielding quest to surpass the boundaries of what is deemed possible.

At its core, the McLaren-Ferrari rivalry is a narrative of human endeavor, a saga that bridges communities across the globe. It has become a unifying force, melding fans from disparate cultures and backgrounds into a singular, passionate congregation of Formula 1 enthusiasts. This community, bound by a shared love for the sport, finds common ground in the exhilarating battles between these two titans, each race a chapter in a grander story of competition and camaraderie.

The influence of this rivalry extends beyond mere fandom, serving as a source of inspiration for countless individuals who dare to dream. For the aspiring engineer poring over race car blueprints, the rivalry exemplifies the pinnacle of automotive innovation and the thrill of problem-solving under the intense pressure of competition. For the young driver navigating the early stages of their career, it embodies the epitome of skill, bravery, and the relentless pursuit of victory against the odds. And for the lifelong fan, it offers a window into the extraordinary, a spectacle of human talent and teamwork that transcends the ordinary limitations of daily life.

"Watching McLaren and Ferrari duke it out on the track is about more than just racing; it's about witnessing the power of dreams in motion," shares a fan during a community event, capturing the essence of the rivalry's broader significance. "It's a reminder that with enough dedication and teamwork, anything is possible."

The legacy of the McLaren-Ferrari feud, therefore, is multifaceted, a beacon that illuminates the path for technological advancement, cultural enrichment, and personal inspiration. It highlights the role of sport as a catalyst for societal progress, pushing the envelope of technological innovation, fostering a vibrant and inclusive culture around motorsport, and inspiring individuals to pursue their dreams with fervor.

As this rivalry continues to evolve, its impact resonates with each passing season, reinforcing the notion that the quest for excellence knows no bounds. The saga of McLaren and Ferrari, with its highs and lows, triumphs and setbacks, remains a testament to the enduring allure of Formula 1, a beacon of excellence that inspires individuals and communities around the globe.

In the grand tapestry of motorsport history, the McLaren-Ferrari rivalry stands as a shining example of how competition can transcend its immediate context to inspire dreams, bridge communities, and drive forward the relentless pursuit of progress. Its legacy, woven from the fabric of human ambition and spirit, will continue to resonate far beyond the racetrack, inspiring generations to come.

Chapter 13: The Checkered Flag

As the sun sets over the horizon of yet another Formula 1 season, the story of the rivalry between McLaren and Ferrari continues to write new chapters, their legacy intertwined with the very essence of the sport. This final chapter reflects on the enduring legacy of their competition, the current standing of these iconic teams, and contemplates the future of Formula 1 as it speeds into uncharted territories.

The Enduring Legacy

The McLaren-Ferrari rivalry has transcended the bounds of sport to become a saga of human endeavor, technological innovation, and competitive spirit. It has painted heroes and villains, defined by moments of brilliance and controversy alike, capturing the imagination of fans around the world. The legacy of this rivalry is not merely measured by championship titles or race victories but by the indelible mark it has left on the culture of motorsport and the advancement of automotive engineering.

Through decades of competition, McLaren and Ferrari have pushed each other to the limits of performance, driving the evolution of Formula 1 from a niche racing series to a global sporting phenomenon. The rivalry has acted as a crucible for innovation, with each team's pursuit of excellence contributing significantly to the safety, sustainability, and spectacle of modern Formula 1 racing.

The Present: A New Chapter

Today, McLaren and Ferrari stand as pillars of Formula 1, each embodying a unique blend of heritage and forward-looking ambition. McLaren, with its renewed focus and strategic partnerships, is navigating its way back to the forefront of the grid, building on its rich history to inspire a new generation of talent and technology. Ferrari, ever passionate and driven by the spirit of the Prancing Horse, continues to blend its storied past with cutting-edge innovation, striving to reclaim the pinnacle of motorsport glory.

The rivalry between the two teams remains as vibrant and competitive as ever, fueled by a new cohort of drivers and engineers who bear the mantle of their forebears with pride and determination. The dynamic nature of Formula 1 ensures that while the faces may change, the essence of the competition remains, a testament to the enduring appeal of the McLaren-Ferrari saga.

The Future: Beyond the Horizon

As Formula 1 races into the future, it faces a landscape marked by rapid technological advances, evolving global audiences, and an increasing emphasis on sustainability and social responsibility. The sport stands on the cusp of a new era, one that will challenge teams like McLaren and Ferrari to innovate not only in terms of speed and performance but in creating a sustainable and inclusive future for motorsport.

The McLaren-Ferrari rivalry will undoubtedly play a central role in shaping this future, serving as a beacon for excellence, innovation, and the unyielding pursuit of victory. As they adapt to the changing tides, their rivalry will continue to inspire, driving the sport to new heights and capturing the hearts of fans old and new.

The checkered flag may signify the end of a race, but for McLaren and Ferrari, it is also a symbol of the enduring spirit of competition that propels Formula 1 forward. The legacy of their rivalry is a story of perpetual motion, a narrative that never truly ends but evolves, reflecting the past, present, and future of the sport they have helped define. As the engines cool and the crowds disperse, one thing remains clear: the saga of McLaren and Ferrari is far from over, and the best chapters may yet be unwritten, waiting to unfold on the global stage of Formula 1 racing.

About the Author

Etienne Psaila, an accomplished author with over two decades of experience, has mastered the art of weaving words across various genres. His journey in the literary world has been marked by a diverse array of publications, demonstrating not only his versatility but also his deep understanding of different thematic landscapes. However, it's in the realm of automotive literature that Etienne truly combines his passions, seamlessly blending his enthusiasm for cars with his innate storytelling abilities.

Specializing in automotive and motorcycle books, Etienne brings to life the world of automobiles through his eloquent prose and an array of stunning, high-quality color photographs. His works are a tribute to the industry, capturing its evolution, technological advancements, and the sheer beauty of vehicles in a manner that is both informative and visually captivating.

A proud alumnus of the University of Malta, Etienne's academic background lays a solid foundation for his meticulous research and factual accuracy. His education has not only enriched his writing but has also fueled his career as a dedicated teacher. In the classroom, just as in his writing, Etienne strives to inspire, inform, and ignite a passion for learning.

As a teacher, Etienne harnesses his experience in writing to engage and educate, bringing the same level of dedication and excellence to his students as he does to his readers. His dual role as an educator and author makes him uniquely positioned to understand and convey complex concepts with clarity and ease, whether in the classroom or through the pages of his books.

Through his literary works, Etienne Psaila continues to leave an indelible mark on the world of automotive literature, captivating car enthusiasts and readers alike with his insightful perspectives and compelling narratives.
He can be contacted personally on etipsaila@gmail.com

Milton Keynes UK
Ingram Content Group UK Ltd.
UKHW020632241124
3079UKWH00007B/61